Judson Press ® Valley Forge

STUDENTS, CHURCHES, AND HIGHER EDUCATION

Unless otherwise indicated, Bible quotations in this volume are from *The Holy Bible*, King James Version.

Library of Congress Cataloging in Publication Data

Gribbon, R. T. (Robert T.)
Students, churches, and higher education.

Includes bibliographies.
1. Church work with students—United States.
I. Title.
BV1610.G73 259'.24'0973 81-1605
ISBN 0-8170-0931-0 AACR2

The name JUDSON PRESS is registered as a trademark in the U.S. Patent Office. Printed in the U.S.A.

STUDENTS,
CHURCHES,
AND
HIGHER
EDUCATION

Contents

STUDENTS,
CHURCHES,
AND
HIGHER
EDUCATION

Preface

How can the local church minister with its college students? The purpose of this book is to address that question and to consider possibilities for other forms of higher education ministry in the local church. Here are stories and insights which show what different people in different places are doing, and analysis to provide ways of thinking about the congregation's ministry. My intention is to provide a stimulus for people who want to do more, or to do better what they are already doing. This book is addressed to the people—both lay and ordained ministers—of local congregations. It can be used either by individuals or by a group or committee within the congregation. Exercises are included to help you bring your own experience and situation to the issues. A referral section at the end of each chapter will direct you to related ministry resources.

Congregations, ministry, and the world of higher education interact in many ways, and an adequate treatment of the subject would take volumes. This introductory work attempts to approach the subject by responding to those areas about which pastors and lay people in congregations have most frequently asked. I have chosen to make ministry with students a central focus, but student ministry is only a part of higher education ministry.

This book has grown out of workshops with clergy and lay leaders, observations of what is actually happening in congregations, and my own pastoral experience. In every case where pastoral incidents are given, names have been changed to protect confidentiality. Where there are stories of congregations or pastors, I have occasionally chosen to disguise the names and places.

Students, Churches, and Higher Education

A grant for the writing of this book was provided by the United Ministries in Education.[1] I am grateful both for their support and for the work of many members of that network who responded to a preliminary draft. I am indebted to many colleagues who have struggled with congregational ministry in the learning society and who have shared their findings. Because this book is intended as a practical and preliminary introduction, I have resisted my own desire to cite the source of and footnote every reference. Most of what I have to say is not original, but the responsibility for errors, omissions, misquotes, and misunderstandings is fully mine.

[1]United Ministries in Education (UME) is a nonprofit corporation of eight denominations providing a ministry in education: American Baptist Churches, USA; Christian Church (Disciples of Christ); Church of the Brethren; Episcopal Church; Moravian Church in America; Presbyterian Church, US; United Church of Christ; United Presbyterian Church in the USA.

Chapter 1

Congregational Ministry in a Learning Society

Sunday Morning

The minister has just finished reading a Scripture lesson and takes her seat. This twenty-year-old lay minister is a college student, living with her parents and attending the state university ten miles away. She is a lay reader in her congregation when it is gathered, and in the dispersed community her vocation and ministry is that of a student, learning to be a steward of the earth's resources through her study of ecology.

In another congregation's Bible study class, a college student raises a question: "My English teacher said that there are two different stories of creation in Genesis; can you explain that to me?" The questioner is a forty-five-year-old maintenance engineer, studying supervision and technical English part-time at the community college.

The pastor of a small urban congregation experiences the ongoing impact of the learning society on his ministry during the week. A lay leader can't come to a church board meeting because she has a class. A retiree talks about his training program at the university law school which is preparing him for a new ministry as a paralegal aide to the elderly. The mail contains an announcement from the community college of a seminar on death and dying which the pastor plans to attend. One member of the congregation calls to talk about marital problems seemingly made more difficult by his wife's return to school, and another talks about a son in college. At a meeting of the local ministerium with the community association to discuss the needs of the unemployed, representatives from the state university are present to offer technical assistance.

In a more affluent part of the city, a pastor who was once a campus minister speaks of new demands on his preaching skills. He says, "I have more Ph.D.s in my congregation now than I ever did when I was on campus." In all these ways and others, the learning society has an impact on the ministry of the local church.

Then and Now

Once college was available to only a relatively few privileged people. Most college students were eighteen- to twenty-two-year-olds who were away from home. In many of the old college towns a decaying railway depot is testimony to the shift from the days when undergraduates arrived with their trunks to spend the term in residence at college. The college provided a total community: room and board, work and social life, health care and religious services. College was a place to live, to work, to find friends, and to relax. There was occasionally time for football weekends, for long, quiet walks, and for Sunday evenings of being bored by having nothing to do.

Many colleges were church-related, designed to "unite learning and a vital piety." Christian formation was intended to be a part of the curriculum. With the rise of the great public universities and land grant colleges, new centers of learning were created which did not have a resident chaplain. Denominations responded by building new churches and student centers in these college towns and sending campus ministers to be pastors for young people in residence at college.

For the most part those denominations which went to the campus were those with a high stake in education and with a significant percentage of their young members going to college. By way of example, as recently as twenty-five years ago the Episcopal Church could expect that 10 percent of the student body of state universities would be Episcopalian. At least an equal percentage of faculty members were Episcopalian. Many others on campus shared common values and cultural assumptions. It was only natural that on a campus of twenty-five thousand students the Episcopal Church could build a chapel, student center, and provide a ministry.

Today, the experience of "going away to college" is the exception rather than the norm. The community college movement in particular has been instrumental in placing a college within commuting distance of every American. At older, traditionally residential colleges, the percentage of commuters has increased dramatically.

- Seventy-five percent of students commute.
- Fifty-six percent of all full-time students live at home.

College is no longer the province of a small privileged group, and it is not only for the young.

- Thirty-eight percent of seventeen- to twenty-two-year-olds are enrolled in college.
- One-third of college students are over twenty-five years old.

College is not just on campus. "Brown bag schools" teach college courses during the lunch hour at downtown business locations. Apprentices at General Electric earn credits toward a mechanical engineering degree while they work. Intensive weekend classes and the "extended day" have made college an anytime proposition. One community college provides a class which begins at midnight for shift workers.

Knowledge, education, and learning have become central and essential components of our social and economic system. The U.S. Bureau of Labor Statistics reports that 80 percent of the jobs in our society require specific education and training. Higher education has become a big business. In 1900, American institutions of higher learning awarded 382 doctoral degreees. Ten times as many were awarded in 1940 and *100 times* as many in 1980! New knowledge and resulting social changes require workers and citizens to become lifelong learners in order to keep pace. At any given time, 15 percent of adult Americans are engaged in formal programs of education and many more are engaged in informal learning projects.

The changes in the shape of higher education have brought changes in the church's strategy for ministry. A broader segment of society is involved in higher education and so a larger part of the church is involved. Higher education is more dispersed in the society and so must higher education ministry be. Higher education is bigger than ever, and the churches' budgets for specialized ministries have not been able to keep pace with the phenomenal growth. Part-time, older, and commuting students require styles of ministry different from those needed by the younger, resident students. The community college movement in particular has generated new involvement by local communities in higher education as recipients, funders, and planners of educational services. For all of these reasons, the churches' campus ministry specialists have more and more in recent years looked to congregations as partners in higher education ministry.

Congregations Are in Ministry . . .

Congregations are already in ministry with people engaged in higher education. Congregations minister with high school students preparing for college. Most college students and faculty members who are engaged with the institutional church have a congregation, rather than a campus ministry, as their primary point of contact. One would be hard pressed to find any congregation in this country which does not include the parent of a college student, a college graduate, or someone engaged in continuing education. Every congregation includes citizens and taxpayers, the basic decision makers and supporters of public higher education.

The congregation may recruit students for church-related colleges or be engaged in training seminary students. Adult education programs in the church may draw on higher education resources or deal with issues related to public and higher education. People in the congregation are involved, directly or indirectly, in the financial support of church colleges and campus ministries.

Pastors as well as congregational members are likely to be engaged in continuing education. All are likely to be engaged at some level in debates about the purposes and place of education in our society. Most all of our ministries are in pluralistic settings and surrounded by competing belief systems which might once have had a hearing only on university campuses. Congregations are already in ministry in the context of a learning society.

. . . but Frustrated

While there are many ways that congregations are involved, a sense of frustration about congregations' ministries in higher education and with students may be evident in remarks like, "We're not doing much with students" and "We haven't been able to get a handle on ministry with the college." One cause of this frustration may lie in *old images of what college ministry is.* In one congregation, when members were pressed to say what it was they wanted to have happen, they recalled a time in the early 1950s when fraternities and sororities used to come in large groups and sit together in the front rows for worship. (It turned out that, at that time, the fraternities and sororities got points in a competition for the numbers they turned out to church on Sunday.)

Often people remember their own college days. Some think of the large student organizations of the late 1950s when 57 percent of America went to church every week, and when student bodies were generally resident, upper-middle-class young people from the old main-line denominations. Others may fondly remember coffee houses and civil rights action from the early sixties, or later radicalism, or new liturgies and anti-war demonstrations. In any case, the image that we have of campus ministry formed in another time and place is apt to be an inappropriate model for congregationally based higher education ministry today.

A second reason for the sense of frustration congregations may feel, particularly about student ministry, is that *many congregations fail to understand and appreciate the unique gifts of students.* Students of the traditional college age (eighteen to twenty-two) are in a period of transition, just beginning adult life. They generally bring a new vision to the world, a freshness, spontaneity, openness, and optimism which experience has tempered in older adults. The students' way of expressing their faith may not fit conventional expectations.

I once asked the pastor of a congregation in a college town what in his experience was different in that congregation from others which he had served. He responded with a story:

> "The first day I was here when the students were here, back in September, I was confronted by a student who wore rubber flip-flops to church; except when he came up to Communion, he had them in his hip pocket. The amazing thing about it was that nobody paid any attention. And the situations that I had come from, if that happened, there would have been a great deal of displeasure."

It is unfortunately true that the piety and gifts of students are rejected in the church often when the young are being most devout, as this student was in his own way. I have seen anger directed at students over their offering of a banner in church and music in worship. At times students have been criticized as too radical because they wanted to act on their faith, and at other times they have been rejected as too pietistic because they wanted to sing and pray.

Barriers and Opportunities

A tendency toward like-mindedness in congregations may obstruct ministry with higher education. In addition to the different gifts of people of different ages, ministry with higher education often involves tensions between town and gown, "practical" people and "academic" people, people seeking security and people in transition, life in the church and life in the world, the received tradition and the latest research.

Congregations that want to integrate students into their life need to be open to differences, conflict, and searching. A greater mix of people than ever before is involved in higher education today. A greater pluralism in religious expression is evident today, particularly in college communities. Some congregations cannot and do not want to be engaged in ministry with students or higher education in any form. Some congregations have closed the door to anything new or different. Some are so involved with internal problems or concerns that they have nothing to offer.

The Reverend Myron Bloy, former director of the National Institute for Campus Ministries, says, "No congregation which is not a palpable enough manifestation of the new creation to differentiate itself from (and, thus, at least implicitly to challenge) the principalities and powers of this age will attract to itself the spiritual seekers of the academic world."[1] Father Bloy's point is that any congregation involved with the world of higher education must first and foremost be itself a vital community of faith. From a practical standpoint, a focus on student ministry is not a way to revitalize a congregation as some hope, saying, "We have to attract students in order to have some new life in this congregation." Rather, it may be necessary to renew a congregation's life in other ways before ministry with students and the world of higher education is even a possibility.

For those congregations who are able and want to be involved in higher education ministry, perhaps the greatest stumbling block is the

[1]Myron B. Bloy, Jr., and Constance N. Conn, *A Report: Parish Ministry to Higher Education in the Episcopal Church,* p. 8.

idea that higher education ministry must mean new programs, groups, committees, and a drain on the resources of time, money, and leadership. In few congregations will students or higher education be a top priority for a new program. But ministry is more than program. Many opportunities for ministry are a natural part of life in the congregation and may produce rather than diminish energy.

Forms of Ongoing Ministry

Ministry in higher education is primarily the work of those students, faculty, and staff whose daily lives are engaged with colleges and universities. The role of the congregation is to help those people be ministers by helping them discover, renew, and celebrate their vocation. The church is engaged in higher education ministry through faculty, through students, through the interaction of congregational members with students, and through the witness of the congregation's ongoing life. We begin by looking at these four areas in which ministry is going on, and we see how it might be strengthened.

Faculty Ministry and Lay Ministry

Roland sits on the graduate school admissions committee at a university, supervises graduate students in his field, carries out research, and serves as a consultant on a government panel establishing permissible levels of toxicity in the environment.

Celica is teaching remedial English skills to rural students at a community college. Her strong stand on behalf of quality education for students has caused her to be passed over for a promotion which she deserves.

Doris is a nurse, working primarily with terminally ill patients. One evening a young nursing student from the college nearby asks, "Doesn't it ever get to you, I mean, don't you go home discouraged? I don't think that I could do it."

Sam is the chief security officer for a community college. He is responsible for the safety of a great number of people and also frequently must make decisions affecting individual lives when dealing with violators.

Students, Churches, and Higher Education

> Sarah is a departmental secretary in a graduate school. Although her job description does not say so, it is primarily through her presence that the department is a humane place to work. She is the one who remembers the students' names, and it is to her that most of them go when they have a problem with the department.

Each of these people is connected in some way with the life of the church. For each of them, what they do and how they do it is related to what they believe. But they do not talk about their work within the context of the congregation and seldom find much connection between Sunday and their workday lives. They have often heard that all Christians are ministers, but they do not call their work ministry. (In one survey, 85 percent of clergy and laity identified "lay ministry" as either "doing something at church" or "getting others to do something at church.")

The church is present in higher education, is engaged in campus ministry, through numerous faculty members, administrators, and other workers who are Christian believers. How can the congregation help make this presence more conscious? How can it support and encourage the ministry of Christians in higher education? How can the insights, resources, and challenges of the Christian tradition be made more available within their working lives?

It has been shown that the most effective way for a pastor to help people become more aware of their Christian identity within their working lives is to visit them within the context of their work. The presence of a representative of the church reminds people of the bridge between Sunday and Monday, between what used to be called the sacred and the profane. But the pastor who visits congregational members on campus needs to be aware that in dealing with the same people in a different institution, he or she is dealing with substantial differences. A meeting with persons on campus will differ from a meeting with these same persons held within the church walls.

On campus, people are in their work roles; they are concerned with getting something done. Their relationships with one another are structured primarily by the functional. They have expertise, skills, and responsibilities in areas to which the pastor will always be an outsider and an amateur. The presence of the pastor may remind people of the vision or commitment by which they are sustained, but that is only part of the picture in the working environment. The pastor may support individuals and help them integrate their faith and work; but the expertise and the responsibility for decision and action within, for example, the university remain with those who work there.

With faculty members in particular, the congregation may also enable their ministry by providing opportunity for them to talk with one another about the Christian context of their lives and work. Faculty members are, after all, the experts and often can do more to help one another than any outsider can. Campus ministries have often provided a "neutral turf" where faculty from different departments can meet in study groups, quiet late-afternoon socials, informal luncheon clubs, and early-morning prayer breakfast meetings. For some faculty members, annual retreats with faculty from other institutions, either within their denomination or ecumenically, have been very significant. The impetus for such gatherings best comes from faculty themselves, but the pastor might aid by suggesting it and helping with arrangements.

The Reverend James Lowery, Jr., once said that "a clergyperson's *identity* is composed of four elements: (1) the person; (2) the Christian; (3) the professional; and (4) the special calling to ordination." A similar thing might be said of Christian faculty members; in thinking of ministry with faculty and administrators, it may be helpful to keep in mind some of the different pieces of faculty identity.

Faculty and administrators are:

PERSONS— As persons they have family and personal needs and responsibilities. There are often personal problems and pressures which originate in the work setting. Economic pressures and shifting priorities within higher education have made academic employment more tenuous and difficult than it once was, and the interpersonal politics within academic life can be enormously destructive.

TEACHERS— As teachers, faculty have always been the primary ministers to students. Some are excellent counselors, frequently sought out by students. Within the classroom, no matter what the subject, they convey a vision of life and a model. In the same way everyone within the college, from cafeteria workers to the chief administrator, teaches through the example of the way in which they treat people and truth.

DECISION MAKERS— Both faculty members and administrators are ministers of a vital part of the society. They, with others, make decisions about the purposes of education and who is served by it, and about how and to what end research is conducted.

ACADEMICIANS— Faculty in particular have a vocation to be guardians of the life of the mind. They are disciples of a discipline which shapes them and to which they are responsible. They are called to seek the truth from whatever source.

Faculty members do not want to be told by others how to carry out these roles, but those who can articulate the issues from a Christian perspective are respected. Congregations are involved in higher education ministry when they support faculty in their ministry.

Students in Ministry

Students are ministers both in the church and in the world. The primary vocation of students is in the world, as learners. One congregation found a way to highlight and reinforce a sense of this Christian vocation. On Student Recognition Day, three students were asked to tell the congregation something of what they were learning in their vocation as students. In this action was symbolized the accountability of the student to the community of faith and the support that the congregation provides to the students in their vocation.

Students are also in ministry within the church. Students sing in choirs, teach church schools, and are engaged in other church tasks. Surprisingly this kind of tie may provide an important link while the student's faith is undergoing change. Such young people may want to work for the church at a time when worshiping with the congregation or professing belief is difficult. Other students are filled with a burning conviction and ideological commitment to their faith and want a way to express it beyond helping out on Sunday morning.

Every summer hundreds of young Christians work in Third World countries and in ministries of service in this country. Long before the

Peace Corps was created, young Christians were volunteering for Christian service and they continue to do so. Denominational offices and other agencies provide channels for volunteer service. The congregation can help students minister by providing information from these agencies, giving the student financial and moral support for service, and welcoming the student back with an opportunity to tell his or her story.

Closer to home, students may be involved in volunteer service and outreach projects in the local community. Pastors in Schenectady, New York, helped create at Union College a Protestant campus ministry which is "student owned and operated." A student committee has students involved in helping a local church build a solar collector and in picking apples for distribution through Schenectady Inner-City Mission Emergency Food Program. In another town, Christian students are involved in volunteer service through the community service office of the university doing such things as:

- being a discussion leader for a group of senior citizens,
- escorting foreign visitors,
- delivering hot meals to shut-ins,
- working with an ecology center, and
- helping in a drug treatment center.

Students can be encouraged to reflect on their ministry as students and as volunteers both in peer group settings and through personal encounters with pastors and other adults in the congregation. Many young adults are engaged in action for social justice and these concerns may provide a basis for meeting and common ministry with older adults.

Focus on Personal Ministry with College Students

For both lay people and pastors, individual contact with students can be the easiest, most rewarding, and most effective form of college ministry. Individual ministry is possible in even the smallest congregation, and in larger congregations, personal contact is a necessary foundation for any programmatic ministry. It can be argued that sharing our experience of God with others, through who we are with them, is the fundamental act of ministry and the primary way in which faith is transmitted. With college students, even brief encounters can be very significant.

Recently a large university conducted a series of open-ended interviews with graduating seniors to determine what aspects of college life had been most significant to them during the preceding four years. The majority named individual people whom they had met as the most important part of college. Perhaps for all of us, people are the most significant influence on our lives, but this is particularly true during the college years, and those who have contact with college students may have far more impact than they know.

When I was a college chaplain, a student whom I didn't know came into my office and talked for about an hour and a half about a crisis in his personal life. I didn't see him again until about three years later when he stopped me on campus to tell me how his life had gone since that meeting, and how important our encounter (which I hardly remembered) had been. That experience has been repeated many times for me and other chaplains. From my own college days, I vividly recall an old professor who called me into his office to tell me how thoroughly I had missed the point in writing an essay. His personal, though gruff, attention to me had a profound effect on my college career, although I remember almost nothing of the course content.

In a similar way, a single conversation with a pastor or concerned layperson can have a profound effect on a student's life. As students begin their own lives away from parents, and differentiate themselves from their peers, other adults often have a particularly important significance. What is most helpful to students is an adult who combines genuine caring, respect, and a nonjudgmental attitude with personal conviction and a willingness to enter into a dialogue.

Genuine interest and respect is fundamental to effective student ministry. The image of the Good Shepherd provides an example of knowing and caring for individuals, not simply trying to get more sheep into the fold. So, too, student ministry begins with caring for the person. When we recognize that students are unique individuals, formed and loved by God, we will also treat them with respect. The student is our equal before God, responsible for his or her own decisions, as well as an adult in our society.

"Judge not" is a biblical injunction particularly appropriate to student ministry. Students are learning to make their own judgments and in that difficult and guilt-producing process need more than ever the experience of grace which comes through the attitude of nonjudgmental acceptance or unconditional friendship.

On the other hand, persons who never state their own values and beliefs are neither respected by nor helpful to students. Students will sometimes ask directly, "What do *you* think?" They will sometimes challenge with a provocative statement, such as, "I think religion is a big rip-off!" Students learn through encounter with other adults by having someone against whom to test their ideas. What is most helpful to them is the person of sincere personal belief who is willing to meet such a challenge nondefensively and enter into dialogue.

Individual ministry with students is similar in many ways to any pastoral ministry. To grow in grace, we all need acceptance and challenge, grace and judgment, mercy and truth. The basic pastoral stance must be a genuine concern and a willingness to speak the truth out of our own encounter with God and the world. Ministry with students can be particularly rewarding because they often bring to personal encounters an intense energy, new perspectives, and an openness to change.

All congregational members, young and old, may engage in personal ministry. Parents have a ministry with their own and others' offspring. Faculty have opportunities for ministry with their students. Pastors have many opportunities for ministry, even, for example, with students who seek out the church only for a marriage service. Students have a ministry to one another as peers. Older adults, students and nonstudents, may have contact with students in the context of church projects and study groups. In one congregation, older adults invite students and young adults on a weekend retreat. In another congregation, a woman makes it her ministry to write letters to students and invite them to her home.

The Witness of Congregational Life

For better or worse, congregations witness to those who are not members through the quality of their lives and their concerns. On campus, among the unchurched, what the church does or doesn't do is noticed, and judgments about the validity and relevance of Christian claims are made on the basis of what people see. This is probably true within every community, but within the academic community the following criteria seem particularly important standards by which the church and its representatives are judged:

OPENNESS— Is the church open to different people and new ideas? Are the facilities available to many different groups? Or are the church's representatives closed-minded and the building usually locked and silent?

CONCERN— Has the congregation manifested concern for others—the poor, the handicapped, refugees, etc.—and for major issues of the world? Or does it appear to be primarily concerned with its own members, with increasing the budget and number of worshipers?

EXCELLENCE— Do programs for the public stand out because of their quality and excellence? Can the representatives of the church be respected for their competence and knowledge? Or is the church the province of the trivial and shoddy, its representatives well-meaning but incompetent lightweights?

CONVICTION— Does the church really stand for something? Does its presence make a difference in people's lives and in the community? Is the quality of its life a challenge to academia? Or is it a pleasant club, a defender of the status quo, a place where people may escape from the difficulties of life?

These criteria are applied to the ongoing life of congregations and come into play whenever the church is represented, be it "officially" by a pastor as the public member of a research review committee, a commencement speaker, or a visiting lecturer in the classroom; or "unofficially" by a leading layperson on the board of trustees or a student in a college bull session.

The congregation may be involved with higher education in yet other ways. The following are examples:

- a congregation which is an advocate for neighborhood residents, insisting that the local college's expansion program must be more responsive to community needs.
- a social issues forum in the congregation which studies the role of educational policy in social justice.
- a lay training committee in the congregation which is responsible for part of the education of a student in seminary.
- a churchwomen's group which helps international students and their spouses become settled in the community.

- a professor from the earth sciences department of a state university who presents a slide presentation showing the relationship of Russian geography to the history and practice of the Russian Orthodox Church.
- a university extension program which is a major source of continuing education for clergy.
- a church which provides day care facilities for students at a local college.
- a pastor with library privileges at a nearby university who uses the facilities for her sermon preparation.
- a congregation-sponsored presentation on biomedical ethics, given by the Kennedy Institute, which attracts a number of students and faculty from a nearby medical center.

You can probably add other examples of the ways in which your particular congregation is involved in higher education ministries.

The National Institute for Campus Ministries conducted a survey of how congregations near a campus in one denomination provide ministry to students. The conclusions, here summarized by James Lowery, Jr., in his *Enablement* newsletter, were as follows:

> Rather than having a special ongoing outreach to the college, the best thing the parish could do was to be a healthy life-affirming community. Students would look for and benefit from certain specific ingredients in that health:
>
> *1*) A sense of community and a willingness to draw others into it.
>
> *2*) A really pluralistic perspective on humankind, not just the "family life" slice. A certain heterogeneity.
>
> *3*) Commitment to a life of experiential encounter with God. The guru and charismatic elements, as well as the professional and organizational.
>
> *4*) A lively ministry of service in which many may become involved.[2]

EXERCISE: Biblical Beginnings

"They found him in the temple, sitting in the midst of the doctors, both hearing them, and asking them questions." From this episode at the age of twelve (the edge of adulthood in his society) until the age of thirty, Jesus "increased in wisdom and

[2]For further information regarding the *Enablement* newsletter, contact the Reverend James Lowery, Jr., at Room 715, 14 Beacon Street, Boston, MA 02108. An expanded view of these conclusions may be found in *A Report: Parish Ministry to Higher Education in the Episcopal Church* by Myron B. Bloy, Jr., and Constance N. Conn, p. 8 ff.

stature, and in favour with God and man'' (Luke 2:46, 52).

We may assume that Jesus grew within the context of family, the town of Nazareth, the carpenter shop, and the synagogue, his congregation. In what context do young students grow up today? How can life in a congregation of faith be a part of that context? Do young people today find the church a place where they can both hear and ask questions?

When Paul went to Athens, he preached at the Areopagus, the university of that day, about ''God that made the world and all things therein . . . And hath made of one blood all nations . . .'' (Acts 17:24-26).

1. How is witness made today in the academic setting?
2. For those anxiously concerned with career education, who speaks of ''the first things'': seeking the kingdom, doing justice, and loving mercy?

''Now there are diversities of gifts, but the same Spirit.

''Now are they many members, yet but one body. And the eye cannot say unto the hand, I have no need of thee: nor again the head to the feet, I have no need of you'' (1 Corinthians 12:4, 20-21).

1. What are the particular gifts of students? of faculty members? How are these gifts received in your congregation?
2. What Bible stories, texts, or images come to mind when you think of the congregation's ministry with students? with higher education?

EXERCISE: Engagement in Ministry

GIFTS OF MINISTRY (From Ephesians 4:11-12)

The kerygmatic: (evangelism or witness)

- to tell the gospel story to those who have not heard
- to give reason for the faith that is in us
- to set forth the unique basis for the Christian perspective

The prophetic:	• to "declare the judgment of God" • to expose the demonic and sinful in human affairs • to stand against idolatry, both in the church and the world
The apostolic:	• to call together the community of believers for worship and hearing of the Word • to baptize • to send the faithful into the world in mission
The pastoral:	• to bind up the brokenhearted • to declare the forgiveness of sin • to disciple, counsel, and support
The teaching:	• the task of training and education, enabling members of the fellowship to engage in ministry and live as Christian people
The diaconal:	• the ministry of service to others to which all Christians are called

Taking each of these aspects of ministry in turn, think about how your congregation is engaged in ministry with students, faculty members, and others involved in higher education.

- How or where are students carrying out any of these ministerial tasks?
- How or where are faculty and others engaged in ministry?
- How does the congregation carry out these tasks in the higher education arena?

EXERCISE: Beginning Your Task

As your congregation begins to focus on its higher education ministry, there are three practical matters which may help:

1. Keep a notebook or journal in which you can note involvements in ministry, encounters with students, projects undertaken, and reflections on the ministry. You will probably find over a period of time that you have been more involved with students and higher education than you had suspected or remembered.

2. Form a group of people within the congregation concerned about higher education and various aspects of the congregation's ministry. It

may not have to meet very often, but it can help raise the question "How are we doing in higher education ministry?" and provide mutual support for those engaged in various aspects of this ministry.

3. Begin by looking at the particular gifts and purposes of your congregation, rather than with the needs of students. Those who begin with a needs assessment frequently end by doing nothing because the needs are overwhelming or because there is no real energy or rationale for responding to any of them. If you begin by looking at the mission, ministries, and gifts of your congregation, then it is possible to ask, "How do these relate to the gifts and needs of students and the world of higher education?"

For Further Reading—Congregational Ministry in a Learning Society

Bloy, Myron B., Jr., and Conn, Constance N., *A Report: Parish Ministry to Higher Education in the Episcopal Church.* Newton Centre, Mass.: The National Institute for Campus Ministries, n.d.

"Faculty/Student Perspectives on Lay Ministry," *The NICM Journal for Jews and Christians,* vol. 5, no. 2 (Spring, 1980).

Westerhoff, John H., III, ed., *The Church's Ministry in Higher Education.* Available from the United Ministries in Education, c/o Educational Ministries Communication Office, American Baptist Churches, Valley Forge, PA 19481. $3. A collection of papers from a conference held at Duke Divinity School, January 27-29, 1978, addressing a wide range of policy issues concerning the church's ministry in higher education today.

"Why Should Higher Education Be a Special Concern for Jews and Christians?" *The NICM Journal for Jews and Christians,* vol. 1, no. 1 (Winter, 1976).

Chapter 2

Understanding Young College Students

A first concern of most congregations in higher education ministry is with young college students between the ages of seventeen and twenty-two. These people—beyond high school but somehow not quite adults—often don't seem to fit into congregational life, or their participation is erratic. Pastor and congregation seem to have difficulty knowing how to respond and how to minister. The young college student is in that period which Dr. Daniel Levinson calls the "Early Adult Transition," a period of being "in" but not "of" the adult world. This period forms a bridge between the world of childhood and the first adult life structure.[1]

Tasks

The young college student is faced with working on the following tasks for his or her development from childhood to adulthood.

1. **DEVELOPING INDEPENDENCE**—For most residential students, college is the first extended period of life away from home. For the commuter student, redefining the relationship with parents and becoming autonomous is a more gradual process. For both residents and commuters, the task may be made more difficult by the continuation of economic dependence.

2. **PREPARING FOR A CAREER**—Students are not just gaining the skills necessary for a chosen profession but also are testing the

[1]Daniel J. Levinson et al., *The Seasons of a Man's Life* (New York: Ballantine Books, Inc., Div. of Random House, Inc., 1978), p. 71 ff.

reality of their dreams and aspirations. It is common for students to come to college having chosen one major field of study, then to change to another, and finally to choose a third course of study before settling on that one.

3. **CLARIFYING VALUES**—The student finds the freedom to make many more decisions in college than when he or she was in high school. The student must make more decisions without familiar supports and begin to experience more of the consequences of decision making. He or she is exposed to more people with differing value systems and is frequently challenged to critical thinking by the faculty. The values and assumptions received in childhood—whether they have been previously accepted or rejected—have to be examined, and a self-chosen value system must be developed.

4. **ESTABLISHING NEW RELATIONSHIPS**—Despite many attempts to do so, few people manage to take their high school friends to college. The student has the problem of anyone who moves into a new job and new neighborhood, with some additional twists because new skills are needed. The nature of old family supports which may have been relied upon previously are frequently absent or changed; the college peer group is likely to have fewer commonalities of background to rely upon; and the competition in college may make establishing friendships more difficult.

In addition, the student must begin to establish a new way of relating to adults—moving beyond the role of "a kid" in relation to parents and teachers, to seeing oneself as an adult in relation to other adults.

5. **DEALING WITH SEXUALITY**—New societal freedom in talking about or acting on sexual desires has not removed the need for each individual to develop a self-concept of himself or herself as a sexual being or the need to make decisions about what to do. As societal stereotypes of sex roles and approved behavior continue to change, the burden shifts even more to the individual.

All of the above tasks contribute to developing that sense of *identity* which Erik Erikson identified as the central developmental issue of youth. The individual needs to develop a coherent, consistent self-concept related to what he or she can do, a self-concept other people also affirm and reward. Knowing some of the common strategies which individuals unconsciously use as they work on their sense of identity may help us to understand their behavior.

Strategies

Identification with parents or another respected adult is one way to define "who I am." "I'm going to be like Dad who is a doctor." The identification often extends beyond career expectations to a newer total acceptance of the values and styles of another. This strategy may make the young person appear older and more mature than he or she is, but people who continue this strategy frequently have later, more serious, crises as they define who they are and what they want. It is not uncommon to find young adults in the church acting out "little adult" roles, seeming decades older than their peers.

Role taking is similar in some ways to identification in that the attitudes and values of another are taken on. Role taking offers a greater variety of options than identification and has less of a quality of permanence. The strategy is playfully illustrated in the film *Breaking Away*. The central character, a recent high school graduate, having gotten an Italian racing bike, not only invests his energy in becoming a bicycle racer, but also begins to imitate in style and speech his Italian idols, to his father's chagrin and anger. When the idols fall, so does the role, but at the end of the film we see him beginning to assume a new role. In college, students may try out various roles—"super student," "college party girl," "radical feminist," or an image of a professor. Role taking is generally a healthy way for people to explore who they really want to be.

Counterdependent behavior is probably seen to some degree in all people in the process of moving away from parents. Everyone has some emotional desire to remain a child or again become dependent on all-providing parents. Sometimes the only way in which people can counter their desire to be dependent is to strongly reject parents and their standards. Mild forms of counterdependency are widespread—students complain about parents and vow that they are *not* going to make their bed, or whatever, because they were made to do it for so many years. Most young people end up, however, with values very similar to those of their parents. Probably the more extreme cases of counterdependency are not found in the college population, because people who cannot relate to any authority except by defying it tend not to go to college.

Ideological commitment provides another aid in making the transition from childhood to adult responsibility. An ideology simplifies the world by an understandable schema, offers clear-cut roles and goals, and provides answers to the questions: "What's the world like?" "What should I do?" and "Who are my friends?" Ideology can be, as Erik Erikson pointed out, a very positive force, challenging youth to be the best, to remake the world, freeing energies from confusion and providing a channel for them. It can also be demonic. Although some are attracted to various movements or find their identity in a particular subcultural issue, present cultural pluralism denies widespread social support to any one ideology other than entrepreneurialism.

Experimentation with various behaviors, values, and relationships enters into many of these strategies. Experimentation is obviously a part of learning to make decisions for oneself. A certain spirit of experimentation, including both a seeking of new experiences and a suspension of final commitment, is common. Students say, "I'll try this, for a while." College students evidence a greater openness to persons of different backgrounds, to different life-styles, and evidence less acceptance of rigid social arrangements. They are more likely than people of other ages to be involved in experimental behavior with sex and drugs and a "hedonistic" life-style. There is what Erikson calls a psycho-social moratorium, a kind of suspension of final commitment and belief which allows personal experimentation. In many residential colleges, this was encouraged and students were in some way protected from their experimental behavior having irredeemable consequences. More recently, many colleges have removed both restrictions and protection, and students are required to be more responsible for themselves in the conduct of their own lives. At the same time, the society tends not to regard their choices as final.

Values and Attitudes

These various psychological strategies of young adults beginning to test their way in the adult world can often make it difficult for us to understand where they really are. Students will appear at times irresponsible, fickle, or extreme in their behavior. Actually, the underlying values of college students tend to be similar to those of their parents 80 percent of the time. Presently, the only major differences between the attitudes of college students and older American adults show up in the students' more liberal attitudes towards premarital sexual behavior and experimentation with milder drugs and alcohol. A very similar difference could be found in the attitudes of college students and older Americans in the 1920s.

At present, young adults (and particularly students who are away at college) are less likely than their elders to be actively involved in congregational life. But at the same time, religion continues to be important to them. In one survey of young adults, 90 percent said that they believed in God; 80 percent said that they prayed and that religion was important to them; 60 percent said that they had thought about God or religion in the previous twenty-four hours and that their daily lives are affected by these thoughts.

Religion is as important to young adults as to their elders, but young adults are less likely than their elders to be involved in conventional religious activities. In a similar way, the political values of students are likely to be like their parents' values, but students are less likely to vote than their elders.

Students are apt to act differently than their elders many times because of the way in which they hold their values, where they are in the life cycle, and their experience of the world. For example, for the freshman class entering college in 1980, nearly 80 percent ranked "a good marriage and family life" as an extremely important life goal. However, few are presently married. Therefore, their behavior is not "family" oriented. A majority share with other American adults a feeling that things will probably get worse for the country during the next five years, but 90 percent expect that their own lives will improve, reflecting an optimism characteristic of those just beginning adult life.

Many differences between the ways in which older and young adults hold and act on their values reflect where they are in the life cycle. For example, older adults in a congregation have often been heard to fault the commitment of young students because they do not seem to stick with something week by week for a long period of time. Conversely, students sometimes complain that older adults are not committed because they seldom give 100 percent of their energies to a project for more than a brief period of time. Other such differences between younger and older persons may be indicated by exercises two and three at the end of this chapter.

The College Environment

The young college student has certain common characteristics not only because of his or her age, but also because of the college environment.

Particularly in the first year, the college environment can make heavy emotional demands. At the beginning of his or her college career, the resident student is faced with the loss of familiar support systems, leaving family and friends to make the transition to a new environment. Expectations for personal and social success are usually heavy. Even well-prepared students are likely to find the work and competition more demanding than expected. Many students find during their first year that their abilities and interests are not really suited to their chosen field. New skills in personal discipline, time management, and study habits are needed, while at the same time the student needs to develop new social skills in relating to different kinds of people and making new friends.

Depression is common among college students, associated with the loss of old relationships, fear of academic failure, fear of the consequences of the major decisions which must be made, constricted feelings of having no one to talk to, and alienated feelings of being different from everyone else. Against this background, episodes such as failure on an exam or the breakup of a love affair can trigger an acute depressive reaction. The rate of suicide on college campuses has constantly been increasing, and most counseling centers are heavily booked. However, many students neither seek help nor take drastic action but withdraw; unable to study or engage in meaningful encounters, they may sleep sixteen hours a day or engage heavily in activities unrelated to their major purposes.

Apart from the emotional demands of college life, there are also intellectual demands. The vocation of a student is to study, to learn, to develop new intellectual skills. The average student reads more books in college than she or he will read during the remainder of her or his life. In most colleges it is intended not only that the student's knowledge should expand, but also that new skills of critical thinking be developed. The student is forced to move beyond simple cataloging of what is true and false to deal with a great complexity of information, viewpoints, and conflicting arguments. Sometimes the secure world of "what we know" is deliberately challenged so that the student is forced to think logically, argue cogently, and develop a personal point of view. Military recruits are physically pressed to a limit of endurance in order to develop their capabilities, and in an analogous way college students are pressed to develop within themselves the abilities of the mind. As the young recruit may swagger a bit on his return from boot camp, so the college sophomore may be overly confident in his or her newly found reasoning abililty.

Commuter students, even those of traditional college age, tend to differ from their resident contemporaries. They do not have the same problems of leaving family and old neighborhood and tend not to enter as fully into the college environment. On the average, commuters do as well as residents academically, but develop social skills and a personal value system more slowly. The commuter spends less time on campus, less time with a community of peers, and has less time for extracurricular activities. Some stress in the home situation is likely as the commuter works out his or her need for study time, changing attitudes and values, and new adult responsibilities. Rather than being totally within an academic environment, the commuter's life is divided between campus, home, and other responsibilities. More commuters than residents hold jobs in addition to their studies, and this creates even greater pressure on their time.

Commuters' feelings toward their college are frequently not as strong or as positive as residents' attitudes . Commuters tend to choose their college as a matter of convenience rather than with a strong positive feeling for their institution or its program. It may not be their first preference but a choice forced on them by economic necessity. Commuters are less likely to be involved in student government or in cheering the school team. Commuters who attend less than full time frequently do not even see the role of student as their major vocation. For commuters, the pressures of time, economics, and scheduling can reduce the college experience entirely to a necessary "time-serving" on the way to something else. A common question among commuters becomes "How long do you have to go before you get out?"

In addition to commuters, many other categories of nontraditional young students are on the campus today. Over 40 percent of high school graduates now go on to some form of post-secondary education, so we are enrolling in our colleges a much broader spectrum of this age group than ever before. More women, more ethnic minorities, and more people whose parents did not attend college are now in college. The function of colleges has expanded to include preparation for many technical and managerial fields outside of the traditional arts and sciences.

Today almost as much diversity exists among college students as among any other segment of the population. Some students are academic in a traditional way; some have read Plato and some are committed to a love of learning for its own sake. But careerism and concern for the vocational utility of education is widespread. Many students are people who in an earlier time would not have needed a college education to enter their chosen field. Taken as a whole, college students are no longer a distinctive elite. The young student commuting to class at the community college may have more in common with peers commuting to the factory across town than with age-mates away at a small liberal arts college. All of this challenges our stereotypes and makes it more difficult to form groups or programs around a presumed common identity of college students.

A Process of Development

Because of their age and the college environment, traditional-age college students are in a transition, or metamorphosis, from what is called a "Conformist" to a "Conscientious" way of relating to the world. This movement involves fundamental changes in self-understanding, interpersonal relationships, and the way in which beliefs and values are held.[2]

The *Conformist* style tends to:

- use either/or categories; see one viewpoint as right and others wrong.
- take the world as it is for granted.
- make decisions on the basis of what others expect.
- conform to the roles and expectations of the group with whom he or she is at the moment.
- compartmentalize life, having different values in different situations.
- respect the authority of designated leaders so long as they are personally trustworthy and "look the part."
- want to know what the rules are.

[2]This discussion follows the usage of Jane Loevinger.

- have a stereotyped view of others.
- be conventional in dress, habits, roles, expression of feelings, interpretation of symbols, etc., although the conventions may be those of a particular subculture.

The *Conscientious* style tends to:

- be aware of having a personal point of view, differentiated from the group's.
- be able to see things from the point of view of other groups.
- make decisions on the basis of self-chosen values and goals.
- maintain values, identity, from one situation to another.
- look for the principles behind rules and authority.
- take responsibility for self.
- take responsibility for own role in interpersonal and group relationships.
- seek individualized forms of expression, interpretation, etc.

Broadly speaking, the process of development at this point in life moves toward the individual assuming greater responsibility for actions, values, decisions, self-maintenance, and the business of making sense of the world. The process is certainly not limited to the college years. But a number of experiences associated with college tend to encourage the movement from a conformist to a conscientious style. For example:

Freedom to choose—Hector's parents have for years insisted that he work hard and finish high school with good grades. When he begins to talk about going to college, his mother says, "It's up to you, son."

Real-life testing—Jack and his family have always expected that he would become a doctor, but he finds that he has no talent for organic chemistry and probably won't make the grade.

Loss of social supports—Franchesca has always gone to church with her parents, but in college she finds that there is no one in her dorm to go with her.

Decision making—If José wants to stay in college, he has to work full time to pay the tuition. He hates the job he has, but he doesn't see any alternatives other than sticking with it or dropping out of school.

Wider experience—Alice grew up with a stereotyped and prejudiced view of Jews—"they killed Jesus" and "they have a lot of money." In college she has a Jewish roommate who becomes a good friend.

Critical thinking—Bill has always been a Democrat because his parents are. College bull sessions, as well as courses in economics and politics, force him to look at various political philosophies, and now he can better explain his own point of view.

Loss of innocence—Sheri is a good student and has been a "good girl." One particulary difficult course threatened to ruin her near-perfect average until a sorority sister shared with her a copy of the final exam which had been pilfered from the professor's office. Sheri got an *A* in the course, but she doesn't feel right about herself.

Experiences like these tend to break down old assumptions and test the limits of the conformist style. But development of the conscientious style takes time. Many students are in an extended transition between these styles which have particular characteristics of their own. It is called the "Self-Aware" stage because self-consciousness is heightened, becoming a sometimes uncomfortable awareness of no longer fitting in. There is a need to think about oneself and one's own point of view.

When the power of old rules and authorities has waned, and internal authority is not yet strong or clear, behavior may appear random, "lawless," or simply very selfish. It is anxiety provoking to live without either old sureties or new convictions. Students may be angry and react against the old authorities which now seem to have deceived them. Since the world has previously conformed to their expectations, they may wish to remake the world to conform to their new perceptions. Some may wish to retreat to old securities and tenaciously defend them; others may escape from decision making into irresponsibility or gamesmanship. It takes courage to wrestle through doubts, change one's mind, make decisions without certainty, and come to terms with a world more complex than we had at first supposed.

For some students, the movement out of the conformist style has begun before the college years, and others will never make the transition to a conscientious style. But a majority of students experience some movement along the continuum from conformist to self-aware to conscientious style during the college years. Insofar as this transition involves religious life, it can be described as a shift from an "inherited" to a chosen belief, from belief to faith, or as a change in the dominant style of faith. John Westerhoff has described a pattern of spiritual development common in adolescence and college as being from Affiliative Faith to Searching Faith to Owned Faith. In the Affiliative style, faith is expressed through membership, belonging to a group of believers, worshiping together, saying the prayers, and knowing the rules, the words, and the stories. People in Searching Faith begin to question, needing to think things through, test the truth, and experiment with commitment. Westerhoff sees this as a necessary step in order for people to come to Owned Faith in which community beliefs are internalized as a basis for personal action.[3]

These categories are not mutually exclusive, nor are they useful labels for individuals. They provide simply a way of talking about some of the different ways in which students relate to the church, and clarify the needs of different groups of students. For example, some students want a fellowship group in which there is widespread agreement about "what we all believe." Other students may need an opportunity to raise and struggle with religious questions. Still others may be interested in opportunities for voluntary service to put their faith into action.

Students and Churches

church-centered	attenders	middle ground	alienated

The diversity of college students is reflected in the degree to which students are involved in congregational life. The continuum above represents the distribution from those who are church-centered (about 10 percent) to regular attenders (about 20 percent, not including the church-centered) to those who express active hostility to religious institutions (about 10 percent). (The percentages are approximations drawn from a number of different surveys.) The majority of college students, as the continuum above shows, fall into the "middle ground"—they are neither regular attenders nor are they alienated. The categories are not intended to be pigeonholes for people, but to give us some convenient tags for talking about the different groups of students who may need different approaches to ministry.

The Church-Centered

Some students are very much involved in churches and other religious

[3]John H. Westerhoff III, *Will Our Children Have Faith?* (New York: The Seabury Press, Inc., 1976), p. 94 ff.

activities. A few are involved in new, nontraditional forms of religion or cult groups. About 9 percent of students feel that their religion is the only way to salvation. Between 10 and 15 percent are involved in religious activities in addition to weekly worship, including study groups, volunteer activities, regular prayer and Bible reading, etc.

Some of these students are carrying on a pattern of religious life inherited from parents. Others have newly taken hold of something which gives them a sense of meaning and belonging. A higher percentage of students—higher than the 10 to 15 percent regularly involved in worship and other religious activities—have been intensely involved in religious groups and practices *at some time* in their college career, because many students move through periods of intense involvement with a group, cause, religion, or ideology. However, those who are intensely involved in church life on a long-term basis are a minority on college campuses. Many who are "church-centered" are individuals who have difficulty fitting into other groups. The cult groups have found their most fertile ground for recruitment among those students who feel lonely and under stress. Within the churches as well, it is often those students who are without many friends, without other activities and interests, or who have difficulty adjusting to college life who look to the church for a support group, a home away from home, or a center for social activities.

The Attenders

Young Americans in the traditional college age bracket are among the most religious young people in the world, as measured by the percentage who regularly attend church or synagogue and the percentage who feel that religion should be important in life. At present they are somewhat less likely than older Americans to be weekly church attenders. Thirty-five percent of eighteen- to twenty-four-year-olds attend in an average week, compared with 42 percent of all adult Americans.

The stated preferences of eighteen- to twenty-four-year-olds are:

Protestant	48%
Roman Catholic	30%
Jewish	2%
Other	10%
"No religious belief"	10%

On a national average, up to 32 percent of college students attend church or synagogue weekly, with a wide variation within this figure. As is true for other Americans, those in the South are more likely to attend than those in the West; those who remain in their home communities are more likely to attend than those who have moved away; and those from some denominations are more likely to attend than others. Attendance drops off during the college years; so college freshmen attend more frequently than the average and college seniors less. Students who have left home to live in dormitories at large secular universities are less likely to attend worship services than those students who live at home or at small church-related colleges.

What all this says is that in habits of churchgoing, students are affected by the same influences as other Americans. They are more likely to attend church when family and friends do also, and they are influenced by the expectations of their community. Fifty percent of all American churchgoers are attending the church that they grew up in, and those who have moved frequently are more likely to be unchurched. The task of the "home church" in maintaining the loyalty of members who have become students is probably much easier than the task of the church in a college community which wants to encourage resident students to worship. The college church, no matter what its style of worship, has to deal with the student's perceptions that "It's not like back home" and "I don't know anyone."

Students vary in what they want from a congregation. Younger church members are more likely than older ones to be choir members and church school teachers. Some students want this kind of involvement. Others prefer simply to come for worship and not be pressed to be otherwise involved. One man, now a minister in his own denomination, during his college years attended services in a different denomination because the minister let him receive Communion and remain otherwise uninvolved. He says, "The liturgy could carry me at a time when I was having difficulty thinking through or talking about what I believed."

The Middle Ground

The great majority of students are Christian believers but not active churchgoers. In a recent poll of Americans between the ages of eighteen and twenty-four, 41 percent said, "I believe in a specific religion and actively participate in its activities"; while an additional 34 percent said, "I believe in a specific religion, although I don't actively take part in its activities." From another poll, it appears that 50 to 60 percent of students consider themselves church members, attend from time to time, and would look to the church when they want to be married.

It is important to note that these nonchurchgoers find their religious beliefs are an important part of their lives. They are for the most part neither indifferent nor unbelievers. Many are critical of the church, but most of their critical comments are also echoed by many churchgoers. The young have greater confidence in religious organizations than in most institutions in our society. At least three-fourths have received religious training and would want their own children to receive religious training.

What, then, is the problem? For the churches, the problem seems to be that they can't get students and young people more involved, more active. This is not a problem for most of the young people and students that we have been describing. They share with most other Americans the view that one can be a good Christian or Jew without attending church or synagogue. Most do not make a deliberate decision *not* to attend, but find that other activities and interests are more important for them. Many do attend occasionally and consider themselves members of a church; others follow a pattern of inactive membership common in the society.

The old saying that religion is caught, not taught, continues to be borne out by survey data. For both adolescents and adults, those who practice their religion are most likely to have had parents who are actively engaged in the practice of their religion. Young churchgoers are likely to consider themselves to be among friends when they go to church, while nonchurchgoers are less likely to have friends or family members who attend. Prior attendance at church school is not a good predictor of whether or not people will later be church attenders, and the level of religious knowledge among college students, as among most other American adults, is very low. (For example, a recent Gallup poll shows that 84 percent of Americans consider the Ten Commandments a valid guide for conduct today, but only about 40 percent can name even half of them.) Dislike of previous religious training is a frequent cause of negative attitudes toward the church among youth, as is experience with church leaders who are perceived to be insincere, unapproachable, or lacking in integrity.

The Alienated

You may not find them in a local church, but if you go on a college campus, you are likely to find some students who appear to be actively hostile to any form of "institutionalized religion." They may claim to be atheists or true believers, but they don't want to have anything to do with the church. Young adults who are most antichurch tend to be alienated from other institutions and from society generally, so the percentage on campus is somewhat less than among young adults in general. The alienated are probably the most in need of someone to reach out to them and the most difficult to reach.

Changes During College

Students are people in transition; so individuals frequently move from one style of relating to another. Sometimes it is the most alienated student who finds a subculture in which to live and who becomes intensely "church-centered" in one of the new religions. We have already noted the tendency for students to become less active when they move away from home and as they have been in college for longer periods. As students sort out their own values they may also experiment with other religions and denominations.

Students who have always gone to church frequently find in college that they need to examine their faith and make some decisions about their own beliefs. Others who come to college as conventional non-attenders find that the challenge of critical thinking and competing beliefs awakens in them a kind of seaching faith. Some have been struggling for years with religious questions and finally, finding no support for their struggle, settle for indifference. Overall, about 20 percent of young adults end up with a religious affiliation other than the one they were brought up in; and about a third of those Americans who remain "unchurched" say simply that, "When I grew up and started making decisions on my own, I stopped going to church."

EXERCISE #1: Understanding College Students

The best exercise for understanding and ministry with students is to actually do it. Make some time to find out more about a student whom you know. Plan to listen and let him or her tell you about how he or she sees the world, what this student's hopes are, what his or her understanding of the church is, what is important to this individual.

While personal contact is the best exercise, the following is an exercise which you can do now, sitting in a chair, or in a group discussion. Read each brief statement, and ask yourself (or the group) how your own experience relates to it. What implications does it have for you in your ministry?

College Students Are Real People

I once accompanied a student delegate to a church convention at which one of the older delegates actually patted her on the head while saying, "Oh, how nice to see young people here." Students are often treated as "kids" by other adults and, unfortunately, as "peons" by the colleges they attend. Eighteen-year-olds are legally adults in our society and are more likely to act as responsible adults if they are treated as such.

College Is the Work and Vocation of Students

Students' work deserves to be treated as seriously as the work and vocation of any other Christian. We do students a disservice if we treat college simply as preparation for something else or as a happy "time-out" before real life begins. Nor should we encourage students to become excessively involved in church activities to the detriment of their vocation as students.

College Is a Time of Stress

As we get older, we tend to edit our memories, and college may seem to us a carefree time because we didn't have then the problems that we have now. But the pressures of college are real for those who must deal with them. Signs of depression in college students should not be treated lightly.

Students Live by an Academic Calendar

The student with a three-week break at Christmas may recently have been putting in an eighty-hour week. We need to be sensitive to the academic calendar, to when stress develops around exams, to when the student is free for a break. One pastor found 10 P.M. at night a good time for a worship service in the dorms because students took a break from studying then. Both the student's days and the college years have their own rhythm and transition points. For example, the anxieties of the freshman just starting out are different from those of the junior beginning to question his or her vocation in college, or the anxieties of a senior beginning to look at the job market.

Students Are Busy People

By and large, we don't need to find something for students to do, and most do not make very many demands on the church or the pastor's time. Therefore, when a student does go out of his or her way, for example, to seek out the pastor, there is usually some fairly important underlying need, and it is worth taking the time to respond immediately to the student if at all possible.

Commitment Style Tends to Be Intense, Short-Term

Short-term programs, projects, and involvements work best. Students are more likely to commit themselves to a weekend retreat than to a group which meets an hour each week. A summer's commitment to volunteer service is a more characteristic form of student offering than a weekly pledge.

Counseling Is Uncommon

Student counseling services are used by only about 10 percent of students. About 6 percent of college-age people list a minister, priest, or rabbi as someone to whom they would go with a problem. The counseling which does occur tends to be short-term. Significant contact with students tends to take the form of informal meeting and pastoral conversation. Students don't need counselors so much as they need friends.

Students Are Experimenters

They experiment with themselves, with life, with limits, with other people, with ideas, with roles. Sometimes they may subtly be looking for an evaluation: "How am I doing? What do you think?" Frequently they will challenge other beliefs as a way of working out their own. Sometimes experimentation can lead to guilt or fear. In all of this, the constancy of the church or older people can provide a countervailing security, as in the case of the student who told her parents, "I don't plan to come home ever again, but please don't move."

Students Are in Transition

Their understandings and attitudes today are likely to be different from what they were last week. We need to be sensitive to the process they are going through, and look not to the past and what they were, but to the future and who they are becoming. Students are in a period of rapid change, and their relationships with both family and congregation are changing also.

Students Have Special Gifts

As we get older, we tend to value those gifts which are most characteristic of our own age and place in the life cycle. The older adult can appreciate the grace manifested in constancy by those who rise daily to care for their children and do their work in the world. Students tend to have different gifts. They bring energy and enthusiasm, a willingness to be intensely involved and committed, a fresh perspective, and a sense of the present not locked into the past. They can be quick to question and eager to learn, idealistic and capable of deep devotion. Many are very open to others, warm, and, in their sensitivity to others, wear their hearts on their sleeves. Students often have a reserve of skills and talents for leadership which they have not yet even been called upon to use.

EXERCISE #2: Perspectives

As an exercise by yourself or in a group, consider what differences there are likely to be between a twenty-year-old and a forty-year-old in the following areas:

	20-y/o	40-y/o
Physical energy		
Personal stake in the status quo		
Decision-making experience		
Orientation to past/future		
Experience of limitation, failure, death		
Change		
Dependence on others/self		
Involvement with parents/children		

Where are you in the life cycle? How does your own perspective differ?

EXERCISE #3: Remembered History

A second exercise illustrates the effect of history on different generations. Take a blank piece of paper, turned so that you have a long rectangle from left to right. (Eight-and-one-half-by-eleven-inch typing paper will do fine.) On the left-hand margin, put a star in the middle of the page to represent when you were born. Draw a line from the star across the page to the right-hand side. This represents your life line, from your year of birth on the left to the present on the right. Cross the line at a point to represent your eleventh birthday. Across the top of the page write in the year of your birth on the left, the present year on the right, and the year of your eleventh birthday. In the manner of a timeline, write in at appropriate points historical events, cultural trends, and the names of public figures which have been significant to you in your life.

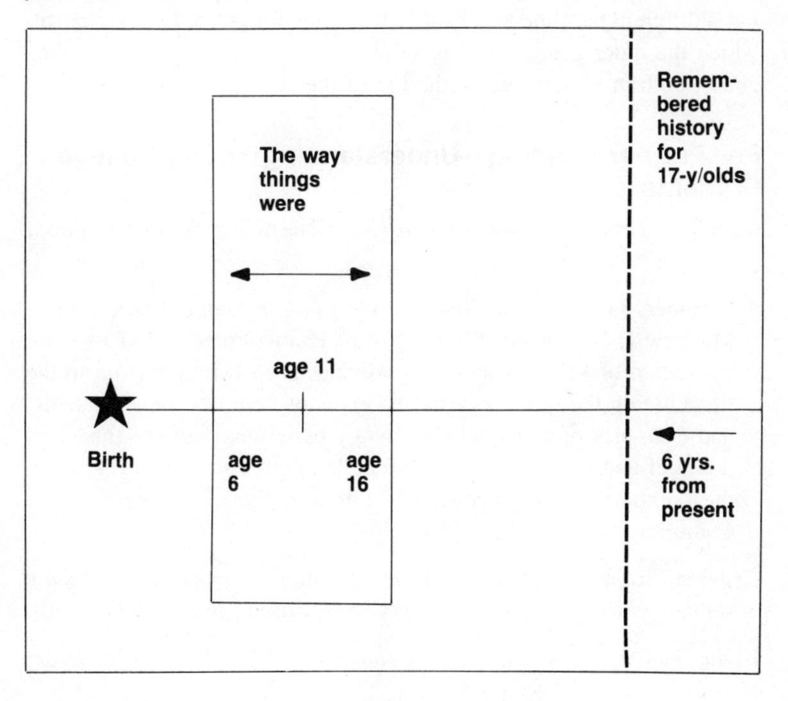

Students, Churches, and Higher Education

You have now a rough map locating your life in a particular history. Age eleven is about the age at which we begin to be aware of historical events in the larger world directly. The events of the next five or six years are what I call "remembered history." Prior to that age, while events may very much affect the course of our lives, awareness tends to be mediated through our families. Draw a box around the five years on either side of your eleventh birthday (from age six to sixteen). The shape of the world during that period probably will always represent for each of us "the way things were when I was growing up." That is our baseline for change.

Now on your timeline count back six years from the present and make a mark. That represents the eleventh birthday of someone graduating from high school this year. Fold the paper over so that only the last six years are visible. Now you are seeing the remembered history of those becoming college freshmen today.

Our historical bias affects the way in which we see the present and the way in which we hold our common values. The younger generation has a different baseline for change. They take for granted some changes which the older generation has suffered through or struggled to bring about, both in society and in the life of the church.

For Further Reading—Understanding Young College Students

Clinebell, Howard, *Growth Counseling*. Nashville: Abingdon Press, 1979. $7.95.

deLorimier, Jacques et al., *Identity and Faith in Young Adults*. Trans. Matthew J. O'Connell. Ramsey, N.J.: Paulist Press, n.d. This work by a team of French Canadians provides a good introduction to the literature on the identity crisis and crisis of faith in college students, and examples of a religious pedagogy based on those insights. It is not brief and is not directly transferable to other settings. (The group these authors were most concerned with were French-speaking Roman Catholics.)

Gribbon, Robert T., *The Problem of Faith-Development in Young Adults*. Washington, D.C.: The Alban Institute, Inc., 1977. $2.50.

Irwin, Paul B., *The Care and Counseling of Youth in the Church*.

Philadelphia: Fortress Press, 1975. $2.95. The focus of concern for this book is mid to late adolescence. Some of it is directly applicable to work with younger college students. In general, it is a good, brief introduction to a style of counseling and group support which works toward growth and maturity.

Nouwen, Henri J., *Intimacy*. Rev. ed. Notre Dame, Ind.: Fides/Claretian, 1977. $2.95. Subtitled *Pastoral Psychological Essays,* this work grew out of two years that Nouwen spent on the campus of Notre Dame. Another brief book, this one includes some excellent reflections on ministry with students by a master of the pastoral arts.

Chapter 3

Understanding Older Students

In 1970, students over twenty-five years old accounted for about 20 percent of those enrolled in colleges and universities. The figure was 33 percent by mid-decade and is estimated at 40 percent in 1980. The percentage of older students will continue to increase rapidly as the number of people of traditional college age declines. Already, the median student age at many commuter colleges is in the upper twenties. Almost all older students are commuters.

Older students include: the retiree taking art appreciation for personal enrichment; the woman reentering college at midlife to begin a new career; the veteran from a poor family given a chance by the GI Bill. But a majority of the older students are in their twenties and thirties and similar to the majority of their younger classmates who are white, relatively affluent, and have better educational backgrounds. Education appears to be at least mildly addictive. The more education people have, the more likely they are to participate in further education.

However, the older, "adult" learners have some common characteristics which set them apart from their classmates of traditional college age. Older students do better academically. They tend to have high expectations for themselves and are highly motivated. They are generally clear about what they want to learn and why. Sixty percent of older college students have goals directly related to their work or specific career goals for which they are preparing. Having already settled some of the questions of "who they are" and made the transition out of their parental home, older students are more autonomous and tend to identify their own goals rather than learning what they are told to by others.

Older students do share with younger students the characteristic of being people in transition. Over 80 percent of older students can identify a specific event, often a crisis, which provided the trigger for their returning to school. Being fired, being promoted, being transferred, having children enter school or leave home, and becoming widowed or divorced are all events which radically alter people's life circumstances and often provide the impetus or allow the possibility for their becoming students. The college experience frequently accelerates change. Reentering students are commonly at first anxious about their ability to "make it" in college and their ability to relate to younger students. Most quickly discover that they can do well and relate easily to people of other ages. This results in a great range of interpersonal contacts and increased self-esteem. These and other changes in self-concept are carried over into changes in relationships with family, friends, and co-workers. Of course, completing a course of study frequently results in a change in employment, either by promotion or career change.

The learning style of older students tends to be pragmatic and nontraditional. Older students bring prior experience to the learning situation and tend to look for the immediate application of what they are learning. At least two-thirds of older students prefer some method of instruction other than the traditional lecture method. Educational institutions are increasingly experimenting with individualized methods and learning contracts in response to the needs of older students.

The chief problem of older students is time. This complaint of an older woman is typical: "Most people in college just have themselves to care for, so they are freer. I have a husband, children, grocery shopping, home, and laundry. Sometimes all these responsibilities are overwhelming." Most older students have full-time work, family responsibilities, and community involvements to juggle.

Older students are more likely to be members of a local church than their younger counterparts. However, the degree to which they are active is likely to decline as they become students, due to the pressures of time. "I'm sorry I can't serve on that committee, but I'm back in school" is often heard. The congregation may need to encourage such decisions to become less active in church affairs in order to support the vocation of older students as students and family members.

Older students may also become less active in church life because they are people in transition. The events that triggered their return to college, such as becoming single again, may also disrupt their patterns of participation in congregational life. As people change in college, old patterns of affiliation and belief may seem no longer to fit for them. The way in which they relate to the congregation may need to be renegotiated, although older students may resist having their understanding of faith and the church keep pace with the other changes in their lives. In the same way that people in this society often look to the college when they want to make changes in their lives, they often look to the church when they want to put down roots or resist change.

Having an older member of the congregation enter college ought to be an alert signal for some special pastoral care. The decision to enter college is probably a sign that some other significant changes have been taking place in that person's life and that more changes can be expected. For those who are married, family ministry may be a special need because the time pressures and personal changes associated with college will put some strain on the marriage.

The congregation can also help older students bring their vocation as students before God. Many people continue to compartmentalize their lives so that their identity as workers, community members, or students is left outside when they enter the church doors. The best way to overcome this tendency is for the church in some form to visit people in the context of their work or studies. Other things can be done within the church buildings. Older students can be recognized when the congregation recognizes college students, and the work of students can be remembered in congregational prayers. Within the context of prayer or study groups, these students can be asked about what they are learning in their vocation as students in the world.

At this point, the concept of adult learners needs to be expanded. About 37 percent of adult education is provided by colleges and universities. Other adults are attending courses provided by their school districts, employers, labor unions, private agencies, and other sources. Most adults prefer individualized learning, and studies have shown that 80 to 90 percent of American adults undertake at least one learning project a year. The average adult undertakes five learning projects a year and devotes an average of 500 hours per year to learning. This is a part of life which might be brought before God in congregational worship, offered, and celebrated. At a congregational meeting or meal we might ask people to share with one another, asking, "What have you been learning lately?"

Participation in adult education may cause people to change their expectations of education within the church. During the fifties and sixties, many new experiments in group discussion methods and experiential education found their way into the life of the church. During the 1970s experimentation in adult education was in individualized education, paying attention to the diversity of learning styles and encouraging people to become more self-directed and responsible for their own learning. Research in the field of adult learning indicates that learning ability remains high during most of the adult life span, but individual differences become more pronounced, making the "one-size-fits-all" approach even less useful than it is in teaching children. As experience and responsibility increase with age, they become more important to the learning process. Adults need to integrate what they are learning with what they already know and figure out how it applies in their lives. Adults learn best when they are encouraged to identify their own learning styles, to bring their previous experience to bear in the learning situation, and to make the pragmatic connections with their daily life and work. As participants in adult education experience these principles in the context of secular education, they are likely to expect new things of adult education in the church.

Older students reentering college say that they need support, encouragement, and assistance in overcoming their apprehensions about their abilities and the new environment. Their requirements for help are primarily in areas that only the college can address. However, 30 to 50 percent of these students also express interest in workshops such as communication skills, career and life planning, value clarification, marriage enrichment, and decision making, all areas in which the church may have some particular interest and skill. However, older students, like younger college students, tend to express interest in many more things than they can possibly do. The areas of interest indicated above may reflect some felt needs of older students to which the church should be sensitive; but programming in these areas may be limited by the time and schedule problems of older students.

Graduate Students

The full-time gradate student is a special case. Generally in their twenties, full-time graduate students differ from either traditional undergraduates or other older students.

While graduate students are sometimes still dependent on money from home, they have made the transition out of the half-adolescent/half-adult status. Issues of personal identity have been decided for a time, particularly in the commitment to a potential career. But changes that may be painful continue as graduate education forces the development of a professional identity, a particular way of understanding and relating to the world characteristic of the discipline. Graduate students do become disciples of their department and field of study.

Graduate students are not carefree college students. They live in a demanding, competitive world. Time is limited, and many hold graduate teaching positions or other employment in addition to their studies. Contacts are often limited to those in their own department. A young doctor, who recently finished her residency in a surgical speciality, said in all seriousness, "I haven't read a newspaper in ten years. It's hard to remember that not everyone is a surgeon or even a doctor, and they may not be interested in how you did that appendix last night."

For all of that, graduate students can be delightful. They are bright, capable, generally articulate individuals. Pastors are likely to find that they have more in common with graduates than they do with many undergraduate students. The educational level of pastors and graduate students tends to be similar, although few seminaries are as demanding, competitive, and as lacking in sense of community as most graduate schools.

Compared with undergraduate students, the graduate students are more likely to consider themselves residents of the college town. Those involved in the life of the church probably have been around awhile. Some may be married and have a family who is involved in the church. Apart from Sunday worship, some things which the graduate student may need or appreciate from the church are:

- opportunity to relate to people of a wide range of ages in the congregation, providing a "real world" outside of the graduate school;
- some small-group involvement which might provide interpersonal support, some serious discussion, and low-budget socializing;
- pastoral care for the family, if married, as issues of time and dependency create heavy stress on graduate school marriages;

- if there are children involved, arranging child care so that couples might spend a weekend together (This might be one of the best kinds of pastoral care which a congregation could offer.); and
- redemption from the demonic myth that personal worth is based on academic success and the graduate school syndrome which can reduce all of life to a game of trying to please one's departmental professors.

The ministry of a "home church" with a member who is away in graduate school can be particularly difficult because the student has usually been away for years and returns to the "home" area infrequently, if at all. But as with undergraduates, the home congregation may provide the only tie with any church. The message that "somebody cares" communicated through newsletters, personal correspondence, or visits can still be important. It obviously takes more work to know and minister to those who have been away for a long time, but even recognition of our own limitations may be a helpful beginning, as is illustrated by the following story:

> The pastor at the church door beamed broadly and said, "Hello, Jamie, it's so good to see you! How's school?" The smile and the question remained much the same on various occasions over a period of six years during which Jamie finally worked her way through graduate school at three different locations and had begun teaching at a small college. During this time she became more and more alienated from the pastor, whom she felt evidenced no real concern or understanding of where she was by his question "How's school?" An honest admission by the pastor that he couldn't remember where she was or what she was doing might well have laid a better foundation for ministry.

EXERCISE: Thinking About Older Students

If you were a student returning to college today, what would be:

A. Your educational or developmental purposes? (What would you want to learn?)

B. What kinds of teaching practices would serve you best?

C. What kinds of relationships would you want with faculty members?

D. What kinds of student services or counseling would be helpful?
E. What kinds of orientation, planning, and advising practices would you find useful?

The above exercise is from the Institute for Academic Improvement, Center for the Study of Higher Education, Memphis State University.

For Further Reading—Understanding Older Students

Glass, J. Conrad, Jr., *Growing Through Adulthood: Can the Church Help?* Available from Discipleship Resources, P.O. Box 840, Nashville, TN 37202. $1.50.

Gribbon, R. T., *Commuter Students: A Challenge for Ministry*. Available from the Alban Institute, Inc., Mount St. Alban, Washington, DC 20016.

Handbook of the Higher Learning for Diverse Adults Project. Available from the Institute for Academic Improvement, Center for the Study of Higher Education, Memphis, Tenn.

Knox, Alan B., *Adult Development and Learning: A Handbook on Individual Growth and Competence in the Adult Years for Education and the Helping Professions*. San Francisco: Jossey-Bass, Inc., Publishers, 1977. $25.

Chapter 4

College Students and the Home Church

Saint John's is a moderate-size, affluent suburban church. Many of the congregation's students go away to attend college. The home folks keep them in mind with a map hanging in the parish hall which shows the location of all the students attending college. During the Christmas holidays a family in the congregation hosts a party for the students, and in the spring the congregation sponsors a retreat at the beach for students and other young adults. Once a year the pastor or associates make a tour to visit students in residence at colleges within the state.

Julie's congregation is small, and there aren't any other students her age. She commutes to college, to the state university which is about eight miles from home. Julie sometimes goes to church with her parents, but not as often as she used to. Sometimes she attends on her own, because she has been trained and is on the schedule to read the Scriptures in worship several times during the year.

About fifty students from the Methodist church in Bristol are in college. The women of the church have taken on the responsibility of staying in touch with the students, and each "circle" has eight students for whom they are responsible. Twice a year, they pack "goody boxes" for the students. The students are sent a special newsletter to help them keep in touch with the congregation and each other. The students are contacted to help plan a Student

Recognition Day service on the Sunday after Christmas, and the congregation tries to help students "be in ministry" during the summer.

All these are examples of "home church" ministry, the involvement in student ministry of congregations which are not physically near a campus. Their primary concern is with those who have been members of the congregation and who either go away to college or become commuter students. In the following sections, we'll take a look at: preparing students for college, students away at college, student groups and classes, integrating students into congregational life, and planning for ministry.

Preparing Students for College

The foundation for the home congregation's ministry is laid before the college years. If there has not been much contact between high school students and the pastor or congregation, there probably will be even less in the college years. In one congregation, a woman said, "We lost touch with an entire college generation after we hired a seminarian to look after the youth group. He left, and none of us were involved." Conversely, where pastors and lay people have been very involved with young people in such things as confirmation or discipleship classes and high school retreats, lasting relationships for the future have often been built.

High school graduation is a particularly important focal point for ministry. It is the closest thing that our society has to a rite of passage to adulthood. It provides a focus for a series of changes in the relationship to society of the individual between the ages of sixteen and eighteen. It is the one ritual which is experienced in a group, with peers, and for which there is public recognition and celebration. Seventy-five percent of seventeen-year-olds graduate from high school each year, and it marks for them the end of the age-segregated life of high school.

While many young people drop out of active church participation before the end of high school, graduation is a time around which congregations can plan some significant ministry.

Some Practical Suggestions for Ministry with High School Graduates

1. Plan a program or retreat to help graduating seniors think about their transitions. Two filmstrip and cassette programs which provide useful resources are:

• *Adolescence to Adulthood: Rites of Passage* focuses on the marker events which may be particularly significant for an individual, and the larger question of what it means to be an adult in our society. (Available from Sunburst Communications, Inc., Room 6, 41 Washington Avenue, Pleasantville, NY 10570.)

• *Life Passage: Personal Growth Beyond Adolescence* is designed to help individuals in a group think about their future plans and passages.(Available from The Learning Seed Company, 145 Brentwood Drive, Palatine, IL 60067.)

2. Visit graduating seniors individually. You can talk about the present or the future, but establishing personal contact will make a future ministry with college students and other young adults much more likely.

3. Plan for others in the church to have significant contact with graduating seniors. Through this contact the young people can begin to experience a relationship of equality with adults. Some congregations have had good experiences with using *Rites of Passage* (above) as a discussion starter for intergenerational groups.

4. If you have a high school group, plan to ritualize the departure of the seniors. Remember the past, sing, weep, celebrate, and make it clear that old relationships end. For their own benefit, and for the benefit of the group, post–high schoolers should not be part of a high school fellowship.

5. Help families recognize and ritualize the changes in relationships that graduation brings. Even for those young people who continue to live with their parents, there must be closure on the old and a new way of relating. It helps when people can name the changes, identify feelings of grief and joy, and talk about new rights and responsibilities. See *When the Road Bends: A Book About the Pain and Joy of Passage* by Karl A. Olsson (Augsburg, 1979) for some thoughts about religious meaning and practical ritual at important personal turning points.

6. Recognize and celebrate the changes in your congregation. Don't

keep high school graduates on "family cards" but make an individual card or listing in your congregational file. Some congregations have an "affiliative membership" for those away in school or military service. Ask someone in the congregation to keep in touch with those members. Make it clear that all adult roles in the congregation are open to young adults.

The Reverend Frank Padgett of Providence United Methodist Church in Charlotte, North Carolina, uses the following ritual for high school graduates in the course of a Sunday service.

RITE OF PASSAGE INTO ADULTHOOD

HYMN OF PREPARATION, NO. 256: "Be Thou My Vision" ...... Trad. Irish Melody

LESSON FROM THE HOLY SCRIPTURE .... Luke 2:41-52

SERMON: "YOUNG ADULTS AND THE CHURCH" .... —Mr. Padgett

RITE OF PASSAGE INTO ADULTHOOD:

Minister (to the Congregation):

Dear Friends and Fellow Pilgrims on the journey of faith, today we are being joined in our journey by these persons who stand before us. They bring with them difficult and important questions and new ideas. They join us with a desire for dialogue and sharing. From among us they may choose mentors and special conversationalists. From all of us they desire and deserve respect and honesty. Will you welcome them as fellow pilgrims and endeavor to live and learn with them that God may be served by our common journey?

CONGREGATION:

We welcome you as adults into the fellowship of this Christian community. We desire to share the fruits of our journeys with you as we hope you will share with us. We will attempt to remember the early days of our journeys that we might be sensitive to your needs and that we might meet with compassion and grace the difficulties you encounter. May the love of God, the example of our Lord Jesus Christ, and the presence of the Holy Spirit guide us all.

Minister (to the Young Adults):

Do you accept this invitation of support and companionship?

YOUNG ADULTS: We do.

Minister: Let us pray—

God of Abraham and Moses, Augustine and Luther, and all true pilgrims and searchers after truth, we ask your special blessing upon these new adults. Be their guide and comfort as they face the choices and consequences of their journeys. Bless the covenant we have made here, that our conversations may be full of honesty and meaning, that together we may arrive more nearly at your truth and may more perfectly do your will. In the name of the Father, the Son, and the Holy Spirit. Amen.

HYMN OF DEDICATION, NO. 217: "He Leadeth Me: O Blessed Thought" .... Bradbury

Providence United Methodist Church honors itself today as it honors a group of fine young men and women who are high school graduates. They deserve the honor we confer upon them by special recognition in this service of worship.

Students Away at College

One congregation has a service in which departing students are given their memberhsip to take where they will, while at the same time they are assured that they will always have an affiliate membership and a welcome in the home congregation. The ritual illustrates the fact that those going away do live in two worlds. They cannot be fully active members of the home congregation, but nowhere else will seem like home to them for many years. Very few students actually transfer to a congregation at college. Students away have a special status, being congregational members who are not present by reason of their vocation. The home congregation can remember them, keep in touch, visit, minister when they are home, provide special opportunities for involvement, minister through their parents, and help others minister to them when they are away.

Since these students are out of sight, it is necessary to do something to keep them in mind. One church has a map visible to the whole congregation, with students' names around the edge, and colored thread running from the names to pins on the map. Another pastor keeps on his desk a separate card file with the names of students. Some congregations list the names of students in the church bulletin at least once a year and remember them in the prayers of the congregation.

It can be difficult to maintain a list of names and addresses. Students are in and out of college, and even for those who continue at the same college, addresses may change frequently. But maintaining such a list can be in itself an effective form of ministry if it means that someone who is genuinely concerned calls to ask the student, "What are you doing this semester? What will your address be?" and so on. The caller may be the pastor, or a designated higher education representative, or a member of a group within the congregation which has assumed this responsibility.

The congregation's way of keeping in touch with students may be as simple as sending them the parish newsletter. Most won't read it, but it serves as a reminder and it keeps the cobwebs out of the mailbox. I once had a student call to say, "You've never met me, but while I was at the university, you sent me a newsletter every other week. I appreciated knowing that someone was out there." The basic message that somebody cares is, of course, even better communicated by a birthday card, a box of cookies, or a personal note. Some congregations have groups organized to do this, or some shut-ins may like to keep in touch with students as their ministry.

Some pastors visit their students away at college. This is most effective when there are a number of students from the congregation attending the same college. What these pastors do is simply plan a trip at a convenient time and invite the students from their congregation out to dinner and conversation. Generally it has proved to be an experience enjoyed by both pastors and students. Lay people from the congregation could also be involved. Those students whom the pastor cannot visit at college can be visited when they are home, and in much the same way. An invitation to lunch may provide a much more comfortable setting than either the parents' home or the pastor's study.

Christmas is prime time for ministry with students who are normally away. Even the most occasional attenders tend to show up for the Christmas service (the Christmas Eve midnight service seems to be a favorite for students in churches which have that tradition). For some, the decision as to whether the church represents a living faith or simply a fable from childhood will be made on the basis of what is heard and seen at the Christmas service.

The week after Christmas is a good time for other kinds of ministry. It is a good time for visits, both because students are available, and because this is often a time of strain in families between parents and students who are normally away. Many congregations plan a social gathering for students at this time. The home of the pastor or of another member of the congregation generally provides a setting more conducive to informal congregation than the church hall. Some denominations observe Student Recognition Sunday on the last Sunday in December. This seems to work best when students are invited well in advance to plan and take part in the service. One disadvantage of this day is that it recognizes students on a day when most of the congregation tends to be absent.

Various other opportunities for involvement can be provided. Students may like to be invited to sing in the choir or otherwise participate in the service when they are home. The congregation might plan a retreat for students in the late spring. Some students may be available and interested in teaching vacation church school or participating in other summer projects of the congregation. Every student should be presented with the opportunity to act out his or her commitment in service. Opportunities may be found locally, through various denominations, and through the CVSA (Commission on Voluntary Service and Action) catalogue, *Invest Yourself*. Often congregations have helped raise money to support students when that has been necessary for involvement in a project. That naturally increases the interest and investment of the congregation in the volunteer ministry in which students are engaged, and provides a sending community to which the student can report back.

Congregations can also provide support for the ministry of those who are the parents of students. In one congregation where few students were available to be recognized on Student Recognition Day, the parents stood up to tell the congregation where their student offspring were. In smaller groups, we have found that parents benefit from learning about the developmental issues of college students and talking about their own children. And one pastor, himself the father of a son in college says, "I know that parents appreciate someone expressing *real* interest in their children. I do a lot of my ministry to students while talking with their parents when I see them at the grocery store."

Finally, the home church can minister to students by sending their name and address to the chaplain or a local pastor near the college. The names of pastors can be found in your denomination's directory. Many denominations publish directories of campus ministers, and the United Ministries in Education publishes a directory of all the campus ministers serving on behalf of eight denominations. If you feel that the student's name and address may not be useful, or may not be well used by the campus minister or local pastor, call on the phone and talk to him or her about it.

Sometimes the objection is raised that students may not want to be found by the church. John Talmage, a former campus minister, tells this story of having received the name and address of a young man with a request to "look him up." He found the address of the apartment one afternoon, and after several repeated knocks, a young woman opened the door a crack. Hearing the minister's name and business, she told him, "Jim isn't available right now."

Some weeks later, the minister was in the campus bar, and the young man came up and introduced himself. "I hear you were looking for me," he said. John says that he told him why and that he chatted awhile about other things. He didn't see the student again until many years later when the student, who had himself become an ordained minister, related that his encounter with John had been a significant event for him in his own spiritual journey, because he did not feel judged or rejected by the chaplain.

Any of the actions which a home church takes to care for its members at college, even sending them the church newsletter, can be seen as pestering them. Certainly a person's right not to be involved should be respected. But by taking the initiative in reaching out to students, rather than ignoring them, the congregation communicates its own care and concern. The student has the options of simply receiving the ministry, accepting an invitation, declining it, or asking to be taken off the mailing list. Even in this last case, if you respect his or her wishes with good grace, you may have left a favorable impression of the church.

Student Groups and Classes

How Many Students?

If a hypothetical average congregation of 300 members had a population distribution such that it was an exact microcosm of the United States population, there would be:

27 members of traditional college age, of whom

13 would be in college.

4 of the 13 would be residential college students, and

9 would be commuter students.

(Five of these commuters would be part-time students, and there would also be three older congregational members involved in continuing education at a college or university.)

If the young students not *away* at college continued to live in the community and attended church with the same average frequency as others in their age bracket, there might be two college students and four other young adults present on an average Sunday.

The hypothetical figures above indicate *one* reason why the college-age church school class is not a viable option in most congregations. A majority of congregations have three hundred members or less, and most have a higher proportion of older than younger members. Often there are simply not enough people with common interests and concerns in the age bracket regularly available for an ongoing class.

Sometimes college students are lumped together with everyone between the ages of eighteen and thirty-five in a "young adult" group. However, this age span covers such a diversity of developmental needs and life situations that it is seldom a successful approach. Where there are sufficient numbers of people, the natural kinds of groups which seem to work are:

- singles groups, generally inclusive of single people from age twenty-five on up, often with an extensive program of social events, discussions, trips, etc.[1]
- occasional and informal gatherings of people in their twenties, including both married and single people, in a food and discussion format, such as once a month at someone's home.
- a college-age class or group where there are large numbers of students available or where a number of young people from a strong high school youth group have remained in the local area.

In most places, the home congregation simply does not have enough students to sustain a weekly class, no matter how good the program or the leadership is. Rather than expend effort on a class that doesn't work, it is better to integrate students into other programs, and if a group is desired, begin with a monthly meal and fellowship. If numbers grow, and the need is expressed, other programs can be created.

In larger congregations which may already have a college-age class, the course of wisdom probably is "don't mess with a good thing." If people are coming, it meets a need. At the same time, it should be recognized that there are probably other students who need different forms of ministry.

In congregations where students have formed a small fellowship group, it is important for that group to be related to the total life of the congregation in some way. Projects for the whole congregation are a good means for doing this. In one congregation, the students took responsibility for an evening pancake supper; in another, the students created an Easter sunrise service and breakfast. Another group of students spent several days painting and repairing a church school room which the congregation needed.

In communities in which there is not a rapid turnover, such groups based on common interests, fellowship, and service tend to retain the same members from year to year as they age. Therefore, it is better if such groups are identified by a name such as "the Disciples Class" or "the Under-the-Hill Gang" rather than as "College Student Class" or "the Young Adults." That avoids eventually having a "Young Couples Club" composed of sixty-year-old widows and widowers, and also

[1]Extensive materials are available elsewhere on ministry with single persons; see the material "For Further Reading" at the end of this chapter.

makes it easier for the young college student who may not fit into the class to find his or her own place in the congregation without being told, "You belong in the college class."

Integrating Students into Congregational Life

Integration means more than saying, "Of course everyone's welcome." With students in the home congregation it means treating students as full adult members, fostering ways for them to participate appropriately with their gifts, changing congregational norms to be more inclusive, promoting interaction between students and other members of the congregation, finding means through which their life issues are addressed, and generally promoting an atmosphere which says to students, "Here you will be taken seriously on your own terms."

The home church is dealing primarily with students who have grown up in, or been teenagers in, the congregation. It is sometimes difficult for the congregation to treat these students in a new way or recognize that they may differ from other members of the congregation. Congregations can discourage student participation either by continuing to treat them as they always have or by expecting them to act like other adults in the congregation. For example:

> Bill always served as an acolyte in his home church when he was in high school, and now when he is home during the summer, his minister asks him to serve again. Bill is aware that people say, "Oh, it's nice to see you back just like you used to be" and that there are no other adults serving as acolytes in his congregation. Now, after three years of college, he feels accepted as an adult everywhere except in his church.
>
> Mary is treated very much as an adult. Although she only recently graduated from high school, she is a member of the Ladies Guild and well accepted as a proper young lady. Although herself unmarried, she enjoys talking with the other women about their children, and despite her young age she can talk about the history of the community as well as most.

Mary fits in because she has totally identified with the values and styles of the older group. Some young students are more at home with older adults than with their own peers. These people are not difficult to integrate into the church (although they may have some special needs for ministry), but they may give the congregation a false sense of being open to students, while more typical students feel that their dress, life-style, gifts, and questions are not welcome.

The greater the congregation's openness to a variety of people and life-styles, the greater its chances are of successfully integrating students. Many needs which students have may be shared by others in the congregation. Many of the actions suggested below would work to include people other than students.

1. **Think "Adult"**—One twenty-two-year-old student received a box of children's offering envelopes from her church. In many cases, students never see announcements from the church because they all come addressed to the parents. List all high school graduates or eighteen-year-olds as individual adults, not family members. Address them separately and include them in all adult activities including the stewardship drive and visitation schedule. Remove barriers so that eighteen-year-olds (at least) can vote and hold office in the congregation.

2. **Think "Single"**—Most younger students are not married. One congregation invited students to a "Family Night" supper, explaining, "Here 'family' means everybody." Perhaps, but it is like explaining to women that "men of God" is inclusive of both sexes. It is better to change the language, and the effort of doing so makes us more conscious of the issues. Many parish programs are so family oriented that many people feel excluded. Try to "think single" in planning programs, giving sermon illustrations, writing announcements, and even in setting tables. A table set for seven, rather than with six or eight chairs, makes room for a single person.

3. **Make Room for Searching**—A forty-five-year-old woman said, "I'm not welcome in any of our congregation's church school classes because I ask questions." Congregational norms often support the attitude that "we all agree, we all use the same religious language, and we keep quiet about differences." Students who are in the process of struggling with their own beliefs often feel out of place. At least one class or forum within the congregation ought to provide a place for searchers, young and old, where norms are "we respect differences, we are open to questions, and we are committed to struggle together."

4. **Practice "Affirmative Action"**—Make sure that students are considered for responsible jobs and committee assignments. Students

have proved themselves capable of handling any task within congregational life. Make students visible in public worship as ushers, readers, etc. However, in *appointing* students to tasks, keep in mind:

- the individual's needs, interests, abilities.
- that most students prefer short-term, intense involvement.
- that one younger member alone on a committee tends to be isolated and ineffective.
- that appointing students who already strongly identify with adults may be counterproductive for the individual and the church.
- that no appointed person can truly *represent* a particular age group, all students, etc. Try to avoid the "What do *you people* think?" trap.

5. **Question "Ageist" Norms**—What might be called "ageism" is practiced when:

- everyone in a group is called by title (Mr./Mrs./Miss/Ms.), except Betty, who is a student.
- Mrs. Brown is allowed to be rude because she is older and has been around a long time.
- the preacher declaims long against the sins characteristic of youth and doesn't mention the sins characteristic of age.

John Westerhoff once said, "When the student member of a committee misses three meetings we say, 'he is being irresponsible.' When the local banker misses three meetings we say, 'he's busy.'"[2]

Be alert to ageism!

6. **Structure Interaction**—One pastor said that the coffee hour on Student Day in his congregation reminded him of a junior high dance: all the students were on one side of the room and all the older adults were on the other. This kind of segregation can be easily overcome in a class or conference setting when people are assigned to groups and given the task of talking to one another around a topic of common interest. One congregation routinely has a coffee hour at which people sit at round tables and spend a few minutes discussing the sermon with the aid of some printed questions provided. Most folks find inter-

[2]Comment made by John Westerhoff at a Ministry Forum sponsored by the United College Ministries in Northern Virginia on December 15, 1979, at the Fairfax Presbyterian Church in Fairfax, Virginia.

generational communication enjoyable and easy once they have gotten started, but they won't do it on their own.

7. **Raise Consciousness**—We have had good results, and fun, using a four-session course for older adults both in Sunday morning classes and Saturday workshops.[3] The basic format is to allow people to share their own perceptions of, and experiences with, students and young adults; to present some information concerning the development and faith styles of young adults; to ask participants to talk with a student or young adult; and then to spend some time talking about what implications there are for the church. A number of congregations have committees or groups of older adults charged with or concerned about the congregation's ministry with students. My experience with these has been that they tend to want to create a student group and are often unsuccessful in this. However, those same congregations have developed greater student participation at all levels because they are aware of students and have more contact with them.

8. **Welcome Diversity**—Generally the more open a congregation is to diversity, to people of different backgrounds and life-styles, the easier it will be to integrate students. The congregation, however, may need to make a policy decision about this. Whenever new people are brought into a congregation's life, there are inevitably changes, sometimes pain and conflict.

I know of a congregation in which a young assistant minister was hired and charged with "doing something" with students and other young adults. She was successful in creating a small group of young adults who wanted to be involved in the congregation's life. The group's offer to provide decoration for the annual bazaar was accepted by older members. But mutual ill feelings and rejection occurred when the group dressed as clowns and brought balloons as their contribution to the bazaar. Unfortunately, this is not an isolated instance of misunderstanding in one congregation.[4] In a number of congregations the participation of students has been initially encouraged and then rejected when it

[3]See *Congregations, Students, and Young Adults* by Robert T. Gribbon, in the "Further Reading" section at the end of this chapter.

[4]Catherine Powell, "A Parish Case Incident," *Action Information*, vol. 4, no. 2 (June, 1978), p. 8. This publication is available from The Alban Institute, Inc., Mount St. Alban, Washington, DC 20016.

appeared that their participation might mean any changes in congregational life or worship.

It may be necessary to work through the issue of diversity before much attempt is made to integrate students on any large scale. One large congregation, which now has quite a successful program of student involvement, spent three years in preparation before any specific student work was undertaken. It may not take so long. The underlying issue is that successfully integrating students into congregational life means neither that "they" should become like "us," nor that "we" should become like "them." It means that we create a climate in which a diversity of gifts is welcomed and celebrated.

EXERCISE: Planning for Ministry

Checklist: Focus on Student Ministry in the Local Church

☐ 1. What are the names of the congregational members who graduated from high school last June?

☐ 2. Do you have a separate listing (apart from their families) for each one, with a current address in your congregational file?

☐ 3. Do they all receive your parish newsletter or whatever other communications you send out?

☐ 4. If you have seven names or less, plan to visit, telephone, or write a personal note to each one during the coming week. (If you have more than seven names, skip to #7, below.) Make a note to do this again in six months.

☐ 5. Next month, repeat steps 1-4 for those congregational members who graduated from high school two years ago. In the following month cover the preceding year, and so on, until the last four years have been covered. In the fifth month, make a list of all the older members of the congregation who are involved in continuing education, and call or visit them.

☐ 6. Keep a small notebook or file folder on your student ministry and, at a convenient time, briefly report to the congregation's governing board on your activities and concerns in this area. You might also be able to use some of the suggestions under #8 below.

Students, Churches, and Higher Education

(For the Larger Church)

☐ 7. If you have more than seven names on your list, find some people to help with this area of ministry. You might present this area of concern to the congregation's governing board, to a committee on membership concerns, to a women's guild or a men's club and ask for their help. When there are some people to help, then:

- ☐ Make a list of the names and current addresses of all high school graduates (and nongraduates) for the past four years.
- ☐ Contact all persons on your list by phone to find out where they are and what they are doing now.
- ☐ Announce the project to the congregation and solicit the names of any persons whom you might have missed (there may be some families who have recently joined the congregation).
- ☐ At some point, make a list of the older students in your congregation and solicit their help.

☐ 8. Some possible next steps for this committee are:

- ☐ Make sure that all graduates receive the regular parish communications.
- ☐ Take a map of North America and put in colored pins to indicate where students from your congregation are living. Hang it where members of the congregation will see it frequently.
- ☐ With the help of young people residing in the local area, plan an event, such as a Christmas party, a retreat in the late spring, or a barbecue in August. Invite everyone on your list, first with a mailed notice, then with a personal phone call.
- ☐ The next time your congregation has a special event, such as a Homecoming Sunday, a Lenten program, a Christmas pageant, a camping weekend, or a parish supper, make sure that everyone on your list receives a special invitation. Have members of your committee on hand to make sure that the students are greeted.
- ☐ Invite those in the local area to take an active role in worship services—reading Scripture, ushering, etc.
- ☐ Call or write the campus minister at institutions where students from the congregation are away at college, and give him or her the names and addresses of your students.

- ☐ If many students from the congregation are residing at colleges within a reasonable distance, provide the pastor with some time and traveling money to visit them.
- ☐ Plan to have every student or young adult in the local area visited at least once a year by the pastor or a lay visitor.
- ☐ Monitor congregational politics. Are members eligible to vote and hold office in your congregation at least by age eighteen? Review your list of names, and see if there are some people whom your committee might recommend the next time persons are nominated for congregational offices or committee assignments.
- ☐ Find an appropriate Sunday in your denomination's calendar to have a Higher Education Sunday or Student Recognition Day. Plan a corporate communion breakfast or Sunday brunch after the service and invite all the people in the congregation who are involved in continuing education to attend along with all the students on your list.

For Further Reading—College Students and the Home Church

Gribbon, Robert T., *Congregations, Students and Young Adults*. Washington, D.C.: The Alban Institute, Inc., 1978. $10. This three-ring, seventy-seven-page resource notebook includes new understandings of young adults' religious needs and designs for training lay ministers. It contains the four-session course "Faith-Development in Young Adults."

Singles

Dow, Robert Arthur, *Ministry with Single Adults*. Valley Forge: Judson Press, 1977. $5.95.

O'Neill, Patrick H., *The Single Adult Handbook*. Ramsey, N.J.: Paulist Press, 1980. $2.45.

Resource Listing, Ministries with Single Adults. 1979. Available from Joint Educational Development, Room 302—Presbyterian Center, 341 Ponce de Leon Avenue, N.E., Atlanta, GA 30308. An annotated listing of materials compiled through the JED partnership of twelve denominations.

Students

See listings in chapters 2 and 3.

Young Adults

Journeys of the New Apostles is a newsletter of young adult doings published by the Education for Christian Life and Mission unit of the National Council of Churches, 475 Riverside Drive, New York, NY 10115. As of this writing, other resources are expected to be published by this unit, focusing on congregational ministries with young adults. *Acts of the New Apostles,* a notebook for young adult ministry, is available from the same source.

LeFeber, Larry A., *Building a Young Adult Ministry*. Valley Forge: Judson Press, 1980. $5.95.

"Ministry with Young Adults." Available from the Judson Book Store, Valley Forge, PA 19481 (Literature Service Stock No. LS14-115). $1.

Extensive materials on young adult ministry are now available through many denominational offices. Inquire.

Volunteer Service

"Invest Yourself," a catalogue of service opportunities published by the Commission on Voluntary Service and Action. Write: "Invest Yourself," Circulation Department, 418 Peltoma Road, Haddonfield, NJ 08033. $2 for single copies.

Chapter 5

The Church in a Residential College Community

Wesley United Methodist Church is next door to the Student Union of the University of Illinois in Urbana, and students account for a third of the six to seven hundred people worshiping there on a Sunday morning.

In Annapolis, Maryland, Saint Anne's Church stands opposite the state capitol and includes within its congregation a few students both from the U.S. Naval Academy and from Saint John's College, where the classics are the curriculum.

In the highlands of Southwest Virginia, a Methodist church serves as the community church for the tiny hamlet of Emory and the church-related Emory and Henry College.

Saint Mary's Church in West Philadelphia ministers to a diverse community of people—black and white, straight and gay, single and married—as well as students and faculty at the University of Pennsylvania.

In each of these very different situations, congregations near a campus minister to those who come into the community to attend college. Their approaches to ministry are shaped by their history, location, and the nature of the institutions which they have as neighbors. Their models of ministry cannot be easily translated into another setting. But looking at some different approaches to ministry may help clarify what makes them work, and there are some learnings which can be generalized.

The extent to which the life and mission of a church are influenced by the presence of a college makes a difference as to the possibilities and problems of ministry. The university or college church is one in which a large part, perhaps a majority, of the congregation is affiliated with the college. It is almost always located within walking distance of the campus, and most were built with the specific intention of serving the college community. Many churches of this type actually bear the name "University Church."

What is called the "contact congregation" has a college in the area. Some faculty and students may attend the "contact congregation" church. It may be the church of that denomination closest to the campus, and it may have been designated a "contact congregation" for students by a denominational office. But the contact congregation differs from the university church in that the college is not a *major* influence on congregational life. The possibilities for higher education ministry are much greater in the university church than in the contact congregation. In the pages which follow we will take an intensive look at the factors which make the university church style of ministry possible; then we will look at the special opportunites for ministry in the congregation near a church-related college, in the urban mission church, and in the contact congregation.

University Church

Saint Paul's Episcopal Church in Charlottesville, Virginia, sits across the street from Jefferson's Rotunda at the University of Virginia. The parish associate has a special responsibility as a "campus minister" but not a separate ministry. Students and faculty members are a part of the parish. A highlight of their programming is a regular Wednesday night supper, program, and opportunity for meetings that involve the whole congregation—students, families, children, older people. The congregation is also involved in issues affecting faculty and university staff and, through a separate agency, occasional ecumenically sponsored programs.

Saint Paul's location adjacent to the campus is not the reason for its successful integration of campus ministry into congregational life. Many churches adjacent to a campus have never developed more than a marginal and uncomfortable ministry.

Several elements in the situation of Saint Paul's help make their approach to ministry viable.

1. *Demographics*. First, the town of Charlottesville itself is of mod-

erate size (less than 50,000 people) and is the center of Albemarle County. Much of the activity of the area is centered in Charlottesville, and people are not drawn to a number of different centers as they often are in urban areas. A sense of history and shared customs add to a sense of community.

The university has a central place in the economic and social life of the community. It is predominantly a residential university with a number of students rooming off campus in the town of Charlottesville. The university, including the major professional schools in law and medicine, enrolls 16,000 students, 40 percent of whom are graduate students.

These situational factors are reflected in the life of the congregation. The community is small enough so that people have some interaction with one another outside of congregational life, and a large percentage of the congregation's members either work at the university or are directly affected by it. The university is not the only concern of the congregation, but the life of the university is more than incidental to most congregational members. In addition, the denomination is strong in this part of the country, and the percentage of denominational members on the faculty and in the student body is higher than at many other institutions.

2. *Congregational Viability*. The congregation itself is "viable" in several senses of that word. It is large enough and economically strong enough to support two clergy persons on the staff, together with secretarial support and a strong music program. While there is periodic concern about the budget, the congregation is not constantly struggling to meet basic expenses.

The congregation is also viable in the sense of being "alive." The congregation has life and energy for various programs, activities, and concerns. There is not the depressed feeling that can be sensed in some congregations, nor does Saint Paul's need to "get students in" to generate some vitality and life.

The congregation is also alive in the sense of there being present some manifestation of the new life, the life of the Spirit. A commitment to community life and the style of worship offer something to those who are searching for new life and meaning.

3. *Leadership and Program*. Both the senior pastor and the associate pastor have backgrounds that make them favorable to higher education.

They see the university as a good place; they are comfortable with its leadership; and they can "speak the language." But the clergy do not attempt to do *campus ministry*. They see themselves primarily as *parish* clergy, and the program is built on the strengths of the congregation. Everything which they do is open to the whole congregation and has a base of congregational support. The programs are not dependent upon students for their success.

4. *Structure and Accountability*. Finally, the total ministry, including ministry to the university, is "owned" by and accountable to the congregation. No outside money or outside agency tells the congregation to be involved with faculty and students. Both the senior pastor and the associate pastor are accountable to the vestry, the governing board of the congregation. Their involvement with the university is affirmed by the congregation.

In almost every instance of successful congregational ministry with universities, these factors are present to a greater or lesser extent. The absence of these elements can severely limit the ability of a congregation to engage in the university church style of ministry.

Let's take a closer look at the four elements:

- Demographics
- Congregational Viability
- Leadership and Program
- Structure and Accountability

Demographics

To what extent is the university an important part of the life of the congregation?

During the last half century, several denominations built churches near the University of Maryland, at College Park, to serve as university churches. But the area has grown so that College Park is no longer a college town but simply a part of the suburban sprawl of metropolitan Washington, D.C. Most members of these congregations surrounding the university work for the government or other agencies and industries. The university community, which numbers fifty thousand people during the day, lives throughout a fifty-mile radius. Three-fourths of the student body and all the faculty are commuters. In this situation, it has been very difficult for these congregations to retain university ministry as central to their mission. A Wednesday evening would find the congregation and the university community drawn in a hundred different directions by the activities and attractions of the urban area.

We read that in New Testament times the church gathered all believers, in each place. To a certain extent, the gathering of the church must follow the natural community; and at institutions which are predominantly made up of commuters, the college community exists only when classes are in session.

Denominational strength also affects the kind of ministry in which a university church can be engaged. Some students will seek out the church which is nearest or offers the most interesting program, but the core of a congregation's ministry will be with students of that denomination who seek church affiliation. To provide a rough guide for planning purposes, multiply the number of resident students times the percentage of students from your denomination times 30 percent. This provides an estimate of the number of students who might be involved in congregational life in some way if the congregation does a very good job. Hypothetical example: 2,000 resident students x .05 (5 percent Presbyterian) x .30 (30 percent) = 30 Presbyterians seeking congregational affiliation.

The actual number of students becoming involved would be expected to vary a great deal depending on the ethos of the college, the region of the country, differences within the tradition, other churches in the community, and so on. But this formula can provide some basis for setting realistic expectations and helps point up the fact that the experiences of two churches of different denominations in the same college community will differ, as will the experiences of churches of the same denomination differ in different college communities.

Congregational Viability

Some congregations are so locked into a struggle for survival or internal conflicts that they simply are unable to minister to others. When the energy of a congregation is tied up in repairing the roof or firing the pastor, these issues need to be resolved before effective ministry can be carried on. Other congregations are calm and stable to the point of death. There is little activity and the message is subtlely given that new people are welcome so long as they do not represent any change in the status quo. But it is inevitable that any newcomers, whether students or nonstudents, will bring a certain measure of change.

Activity and friendliness are helpful, but not enough, in a congregation. A religious congregation exists to deal with fundamental spiritual realities and must at some level offer the possibility of new life. That is a difficult thing to measure. It is not simply a matter of theological stance or style of life. I know of both conservative and liberal congregations in which rich possibilities of new life are offered. It may be simply a case of the Spirit blowing where it will, but a congregation's commitment to clarity and integrity about its mission and life together certainly helps.

Leadership and Program

One minister who is now pastor of a lively and liberal urban congregation attributes a part of his success to the fact that he shares many of the prejudices of his people. Formerly he had served in a blue-collar, suburban neighborhood, and he says that he now realizes that he spent a lot of time disagreeing with people about things that had nothing to do with the gospel. To be effective in a university setting, it certainly helps if a pastor shares the prejudices of the academic world and is at home in it.

One long-time campus minister at the Massachusetts Institute of Technology, who had a notably strong faculty ministry, used to say that he had learned a "proper disrespect" for professors. While he loved the academic setting, he was not in awe of it and appreciated the gifts and talents of faculty while also knowing their shortcomings, conceits, and prejudices. Not everyone who ministers in the university setting needs a Ph.D. any more than hospital chaplains need an M.D. What is necessary is an appreciation of academic life, a commitment to its purposes, and a confidence about one's own gifts and competence in that setting.

The specifics of program in university congregations vary with the peculiar gifts of the clergy and congregation and the opportunities which are available. One congregation, near the College of William and Mary in historic Williamsburg, has a number of students involved in a service of evensong late Sunday afternoon. Seventy students are involved in the evensong choir. The service draws on the resources of strong music programs in the church and college. Also, in that particular setting, Sunday afternoon is when the tourists have gone, and local residents and students can put the historic setting to their own uses. Another congregation which has good facilities in the center of an urban campus runs a lunch program each weekday noon.

Both of these are examples of programs which might not happen if the students were not present, but they build on the unique gifts and opportunities of the congregation and they are not foreign to its life. Other congregations are simply intentional about having programs in which students, as well as other congregational members, may comfortably participate. The list includes a meditation group, a world hunger program, church school classes, a drama group, choirs, a Seder meal, early weekday services, and so on.

Programs may also include volunteer service where this is an ongoing part of life in the congregation. Students have demonstrated their willingness to work with retarded children, sort trash at a recycling center, visit hospitals, collect food for a soup kitchen, and much more. University churches involved in such ministries have found students willing to help. It is much easier for students to get involved in projects when congregational members with a longer tenure in the community have done the organizational work. Of course, it's not surprising if students don't volunteer in congregations where no one else does either.

Another form of outreach is to offer programs to which the entire university community is invited, based on some special gift of the congregation. One church has a magnificent organ and offers concerts for the community. Another has a small endowment fund which is used to bring in an occasional lecturer. A key element, as one university pastor puts it, is "we don't do much, but we try to do it with excellence."

Structure and Accountability

It is easy for a congregation not to be involved in university ministry. Many churches sit opposite colleges and have no involvement other than with a few faculty families who may attend. Congregations which do manage an effective "university church" style of ministry have made an intentional commitment to that as their mission.

Such commitment is not without cost. In hearing the stories of university churches, it is not uncommon to hear, "We lost some people over the Vietnam issue" or "Well, many members left in the early sixties when we were struggling over civil rights, and the congregation we have now has all come since then." Churches which are involved with a college population tend to get involved with issues, new people, new styles, change, and conflict. In contrast, congregations which have chosen to "keep the peace" or defend the status quo tend to attract leadership which will guarantee noninvolvement.

Few of us have as much enthusiasm for a task laid on us as for one we have chosen or to which we have been called. The same is true of congregations. University church ministry is somewhat limited when it is a mission assigned by a higher judicatory. Sometimes this occurs when a campus minister is assigned an office in the church building but is paid by and accountable to someone else. The result is often continuing conflict, confusion about priorities, resentment, and a feeling on the part of the congregation, "Let George (or whoever) do it; he's paid to worry about the students—but leave us alone."

Congregational ministry needs to be a congregational decision and responsibility. College Avenue Church at Ball State University (Muncie, Indiana) shares a building and cooperates with the Wesley Foundation, but the pastor and congregation have thought through their own rationale and methods for a ministry with students. That rationale, in outline, is as follows:

A. Theological
   1. The Church is the Body of Christ.
   2. The Church is the People of God.
   3. The Church gathers and sends
   4. All Christians are called to ministry.

B. Practical
   1. The Campus Ministry needs the resources of the congregation.
   2. The Church benefits from the involvement of the students.
   3. At Ball State we share a building together.

C. Missional
   1. The Church is the place to teach discipleship.
   2. The students keep the Church open to the university.
   3. Students in the 1980s will trust the Church in a new way.
   4. We've asked students to live down to our expectations long enough.

The content of this particular rationale is less important than the fact of having developed one. In the process, the congregation surfaced and worked with some of their images of the past and the present, conflicts felt in sharing the building with the Wesley Foundation, and resistances to change within the congregation. The pastor says, "History is important. It has to do with the images which people have." In every university congregation there is a history of people remembered—good and bad times, what used to happen—that often needs to be surfaced and celebrated or exorcised before people can deal with the present opportunities for mission.

As is evidenced in the "Missional" section of the rationale, College Avenue Church understands its mission as encouraging and teaching church membership for students. The congregation is very intentional in carrying out this task. Members of the congregation greet students visiting the church and ask them to sign the guest register. Although it is recognized that "a student who attends ten times a year is very active," all students are offered affiliate membership in the congregation. Students who have signed the guest register are put on the congregation's mailing list and sent personal letters during Advent and Lent and during the summer.

The church program includes many ways for students to be involved, including: groups for study, for prayer, and for drama; a guitar class; house groups; a group for pre-seminary students; and a married students' group. Community dinners, the church's choirs, and work camps also provide opportunities for involvement. Students are recruited for leadership in other programs of the congregation and encouraged to be emissaries for the church in inviting other students to participate. This is the primary means through which new students come into College Avenue Church, although students are also kept aware of the church through advertisements in the campus newspaper and mass mailings sent to Methodist students.

Although College Avenue Church has a very different style of ministry from Saint Paul's in Charlottesville, many of the factors which make for their successes are similar. Muncie, Indiana, is a town of about seventy-five thousand, the county seat and only city in Delaware County, located about fifty miles from the outskirts of Indianapolis. Ball State University is a significant part of the life of Muncie, enrolling about seventeen thousand students. College Avenue Church was built adjacent to the campus, has a fifty-year history of involvement, and draws a major part of its congregation from the university faculty and staff. Both clergy and lay leadership are committed to student ministry, but this would be a strong and lively congregation even without the students.

The College Avenue Church ministry is focused on something which the congregation is committed to and does well—helping people exercise church membership—and this ministry is very effective with that percentage of students who might be expected to attend church. A little over 10 percent of the student body is Methodist, and just about 30 percent of these students (six hundred a year) find College Avenue United Methodist Church. Levels of participation vary, but on an average Sunday when the university is in session, there will be around two hundred students worshiping with the congregation. The congregation is not involved in other forms of ministry to the campus or to the students who do not attend, but leaves that ministry to the Methodist Wesley Foundation. Again, the congregation's staff members see themselves as *parish* ministers and are not attempting to do the job of the *campus* minister.

Other Congregations in a College Community

The Church-Related College

If you are the pastor of a local Baptist congregation located three miles down the road from a small Roman Catholic school, the task may be pretty clear. You visit the administration, arrange to provide pastoral care and perhaps Sunday transportation for any Baptist students, and offer to present a Baptist perspective when it would be appropriate. What do you do if you are the pastor of a Presbyterian church located on the campus of a Presbyterian college, and there are six ordained ministers with Ph.D.s in your congregation?

The situation of the denominational church at a denominational college helps illustrate the fact that there are different functions which the two perform. The professor of religion at the college sits in the congregation as a worshiper to hear and respond to the proclaimed Word. His action and response as a worshiper may also (we hope) affect his life and work as a teacher and critical scholar of that word. In Anderson, Indiana, there are eight congregations of the Church of God and a denominational college. Park Place Church is located right across the street from the college and the active campus ministry office of the college. Yet, the church has a lively and intentional program to involve students in church school, worship, a special Wednesday night forum, a prayer group, and opportunities for service. This is all a part of the educational program of the congregation which takes place in the context of a worshiping community and is intended to nurture Christian belief and practice.

The special tension for the denominational church near a denominational college is both to recognize and to respect the roles of both institutions. The congregation must insist that it does have a unique role and ministry and encourage the college in its role of promoting learning, critical thinking, and sound scholarship.

The Urban Mission Congregation

In Old First Church, the drama group is practicing a play about sexual liberation while an old man who has come in off the street sleeps off a hangover in the back pew. Downstairs, elderly residents of the community are being served a hot lunch while a student posts a notice for a nuclear disarmament rally.

In a number of urban areas, congregations like Old First have a particular commitment to be involved in their communities, to welcome the dispossessed, to be open to controversial issues. They are frequently involved in new forms of liturgical practice, use of the arts in worship, and strong lay involvement in all phases of their life. They generally have a strong sense of the religious reasons for their involvement and find communal worship and discipline central in their lives.

The usual story of such congregations is that they were reborn from institutional death: a large traditional congregation gradually moved away or passed away, leaving a few members and a building in a radically changed neighborhood. Then, when nothing else could be done, a pastor was called or appointed who was committed to involvement with the neighborhood and a vision of what the church might be.

Such congregations play a special role in higher education ministry. Some are located near universities or in low-rent districts where students live; in other cases, some students will find their way across town to be involved. These congregations often attract students who would not be reached by many traditional congregations: student activists, homosexuals, artists, and others who feel alienated from traditional churches. These congregations also frequently provide a witness, by their highly visible and often controversial involvements, to many non-attending students whose criticisms of the church are that it is uninvolved, irrelevant, and committed to the status quo.

The Contact Congregations

Contact congregations frequently have a series of problems when it comes to student ministry. Such congregations often find that:

- the church building is located a mile or more from the campus;
- less than 10 percent of congregational members have an involvement with the college;
- the pastor has no particular skill or interest in academic ministries;
- the energy of the congregation is heavily invested in ministry with other constituencies, community projects, or internal issues.

And yet the congregation finds that it has a responsibility for ministry with students because:

- it is the only or nearest congregation of that denomination;
- a few students occasionally seek it out;
- the denomination's regional office has asked it to assume a responsibility for "campus ministry."

Pastors and congregations in this situation frequently experience some frustration and guilt about their ministry, which can be alleviated by accepting the problem. This means, first of all, having the congregation or governing board decide whether or not to accept the responsibility which may seem thrust upon them. (One rationale might be, "We have a ministry to the 'stranger within our gates.'") Then some decisions can be made about the purposes of the ministry and the amount of time, energy, and attention it should receive. Student ministry will very seldom be a top priority in the contact congregation, but if some decisions are made about what can reasonably be done, the pastor and congregation can feel positive about their work rather than feel the burden of having failed to do everything.

Precisely because it is not a high priority and visible ministry, it may be well to remind the congregation of its special calling just before students return. The contact congregation has in one sense a task the reverse of the "home church." It is called to extend hospitality to students who have not been part of its life, who will probably not transfer into membership, who are transients, and who will frequently be somewhere else. But some of the attitudes and activities of the "home church" seeking to integrate students into full participation will be important for the contact congregation also. The contact congregation is also probably the "home church" for other students, and a "ministry to our own" can complement and reinforce a "ministry to the stranger."

The contact congregation is going to be ministering primarily to the "affiliative student," those who are churchgoers and for whom congregational involvement has some importance. Students are most likely to come in the first few weeks of their freshman year and may be looking for some sense of "home away from home" in a difficult period of transition.

It won't be like home because the place is different, they don't know anyone, and the style of worship is different. Particularly in the first few weeks of the fall semester, some of the things which may be helpful are:

- people at the door to greet and welcome students on Sunday morning, particularly other students or faculty members.
- bulletins or worship leaflets in the pews which are easy for people who are unfamiliar with the service to follow.
- a public welcome to students from the pastor, perhaps extending an offer for students to become associate members.
- a Sunday brunch following the service at which students can meet other students and a few other members of the congregation. (If you invite the whole congregation, the newcomers get lost.)

Beyond welcoming and inviting students to participate in programs, how does the church make itself available to those students who may need to seek it out at other times? Their numbers are few, but often they are the ones with the greatest needs. A church could do the following:

- make it easy to find the church office and to leave a message;
- establish a scheduled time when "the pastor is in" (perhaps after a weekday service); and
- identify the names of faculty members in the congregation who are willing to have students contact them on campus.

Students, Churches, and Higher Education

The ministry of a contact congregation can be made broader and more effective through involvement with other networks, such as ministers on campus, denominational higher education networks, other churches of the denomination in the area, community clergy associations, other community agencies, prayer breakfasts, etc.

If there are campus ministers of other denominations working on the campus, it is well worthwhile for the local church pastor to meet with them from time to time. Usually the campus minister(s) will be glad to have the contact and will be happy to help orient the pastor to the campus, refer students of that denomination, help publicize the presence of the contact congregation, provide a place to meet students on campus, keep the pastor informed as to what is happening on campus, and welcome participation in ecumenical activities. Some colleges will recognize the pastor of a contact congregation as an associate campus minister and provide the names of students who have indicated that denominational preference.

Campus ministers of your own denomination on other campuses can also be a useful resource. Even if they are some distance away, call and ask if there are any retreats or conferences for faculty or students which you might publicize in your congregation. Find out how to be in touch with your denominational office for higher education ministry and what resources or publications are available. Invite the campus minister to come and preach sometime.

In some situations, several churches of a common tradition can share a ministry. In Durham, North Carolina, there are five Lutheran churches (representing three national Lutheran synods), each with a membership between 100 and 400, and two universities with a combined enrollment of 13,000, but only 170 students who list "Lutheran" as their religious preference. The five congregations established a council composed of the pastor and two lay people from each congregation which meets three times a year with Lutheran students. The congregations have aided the students by providing some money for a newsletter, some assistance and leadership for student retreats, and a fall gathering at one of the churches. Each congregation has a special Student Sunday once during the academic year to which all Lutheran students are invited, to introduce them to a diversity of styles of congregational life and worship. The students, in turn, have developed and presented several adult education courses, dramatic presentations, and musical offerings in the churches.

This model of interchurch cooperation allows congregations with limited resources to meet a diversity of student needs and to gain some mutual support for their own ministries and support for a student group, all with a very limited number of dollars, meetings, and people.

Ecumenical cooperation can provide another avenue and source of support for the congregation's ministry with higher education. In Morgantown, West Virginia, churches of five denominations and the University Christian Council jointly produced a "Learning for Living School" on four successive Wednesday evenings. Five educational programs were run simultaneously for the congregations and college community. Topics included "Contemporary Theological Trends," "Prayer and Spiritual Disciplines," "Housing in Morgantown," "The Bible—What Do We Think of It Now?" and a music workshop. Each week the topics were addressed by presenters from different faith traditions and different areas of expertise.

Congregations involved with projects in their community may naturally find themselves involved with the local college as well. For example, congregations sponsoring a summer recreation program for disadvantaged youth found an ally in the physical education department of the state university nearby; a pastor concerned with prisoners in the county detention center found that the college was willing to offer an extension program in the jail; a community ministry working with tenants of a housing project arranged for college staff to provide needed expertise; a weekly prayer breakfast meets in a college dining room and includes some faculty and administrators as well as community leaders (these meetings frequently provide a forum for the discussion of community issues).

The Reverend J Springer, an American Baptist minister working with the United Ministries in Education, has developed a simple method which has been used extensively to initiate cooperation between colleges and the religious leadership in local communities. Results of such cooperation have included joint sponsorship of programs by churches and colleges, the presence of local clergy in classrooms when topics related to religion arise, training courses in career counseling for local clergy, and the development of special services such as day care where needed. The existence of good working relationships between the college and the local religious community has also proved valuable when questions arise in the community about college policies or incidents involving students. This means of extending the ministry of the congregation is described in greater detail in chapter 7.

EXERCISE: How Near Is Near?

Sometimes the geographical proximity of church and campus buildings doesn't reflect the actual proximity of congregation and college. Think of the congregation and college as relationships of people, some very much involved and some on the periphery. You could draw concentric circles like so:

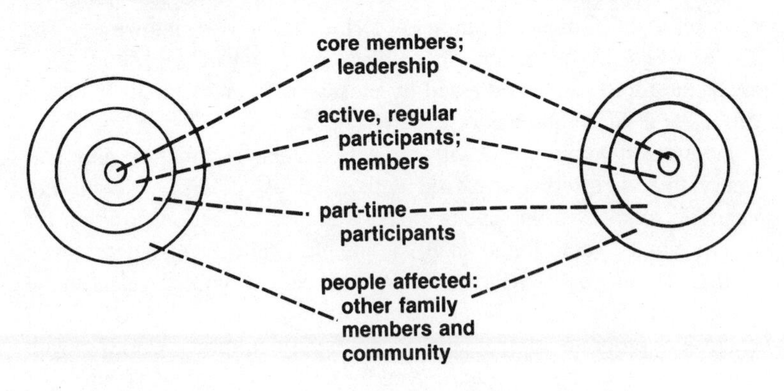

Now think about your congregation and the local college:

- Are there people in the congregation who are also involved in the college?
- How involved are they in the college? In the congregation?
- Are there active members of your congregation who are also active members of the college community?
- Thinking about people, rather than geography, how close to the college is the congregation? Where might you build some bridges?
- Make a list of all the people in the congregation who are involved in any way with the college, and keep adding to it.

EXERCISE: The Mission of the Church

Here are parts of two public statements from congregations near universities that try to summarize briefly the congregation's self-understanding:

"The Church is called to respond to student needs, both spoken and unspoken, with the only real answer to their deepest desires—the love and saving grace of Jesus Christ . . . Broadway University Ministries is based on the conviction that the Christian faith is to be examined as well as lived . . . students are challenged to follow Jesus Christ and to understand how the Christian faith relates to social, political and personal questions. . . ."

"At the center of our community life is the weekly celebration of the Resurrection . . . this great act of thanksgiving and commitment informs, nourishes, and directs all the other activities and encounters of our lives . . . it is in His name, and love, that all of us, laity and clergy alike, learn to minister in our several vocations . . . (St. Paul's was established to be) a home where people, especially students, would be challenged intellectually and spiritually as they continued in, or perhaps, began their spiritual journeys . . . St. Paul's primary purpose is still to witness to, and to strengthen Christian faith and commitment at the University of Virginia."

Does your congregation have a statement of mission? What does this say about who you are to students or to the college community? What would you want to say about your congregation?

For Further Reading—The Church in a Residential College Community

"Case Studies: Parish and Synagogue Ministries to Higher Education," *The NICM Journal for Jews and Christians,* vol. 4, no. 4 (Fall, 1979).

"Interact: Case Studies in Town/Gown Ministry." Available from the United Ministries in Education Communication Office, % Educational Ministries, American Baptist Churches, Valley Forge, PA 19481.

Springer, J, *Handbook/Tool Kit*. The *Handbook/Tool Kit* may be secured by sending a two-dollar check (payable to J Springer) to J Springer, Church Hill Road, R.D. 3, Dalton, PA 18414.

See also resources following "Partnerships with Campus Ministry," chapter 8.

Chapter 6

Community College and Local Church

The community college is a different kind of entity. It has been compared to:

- a supermarket, because people can go and select what they want from a variety of offerings;
- a factory, mass-producing education, to which people go to work in the morning and return home from at night or are educated on the swing shift;
- a clinic, offering remedial education in local neighborhoods;
- an education escalator, which people get on and off at will, engaging in lifelong learning;
- an extended high school, teaching grades 13 and 14.

Each of these analogies may illuminate something about the community college, but they do not accurately describe it. We would perhaps understand the community college better if it were called a "postsecondary educational service agency," avoiding the term "college" altogether.

This agency is designed to provide educational services to local communities throughout the United States. It is intended that postsecondary educational services be within commuting distance of every citizen. The goals of the community college are to bring educational resources to bear as needed on a wide variety of community problems and needs, to provide the technical training necessary for people to work for the various industries and other employers in their local area, and to serve as an easily accessible entry point for further education by offering the first two years of an undergraduate education. While the goals of this agency are national in scope, community colleges are not part of a federal bureaucracy. Local control is an important element of this system, with some community colleges having local boards of trustees and some being part of a state system with extensive local advisory committees. To keep in mind the unique nature of this agency, try to read "communitycollege" as one word.

Looks can be deceiving. The community college may look like a typical college when it has a pleasant green campus on the outskirts of town with young students coming and going to classes during the day. What you don't see are the classes being offered at twenty different locations around the county, the second shift of students on campus until late in the evening, or the meetings with business leaders and other agencies. In some places the community college doesn't have a campus but operates in a number of different locations; or in urban areas the "campus" may be located within a downtown office tower.

On-campus ministries with students at community colleges are limited. Students come to classes for part of a day and then immediately leave for their jobs or other responsibilities. Some students rarely come to the "main campus," and even on campus there may be no place to meet. One campus minister at a community college with no lounges or cafeteria spends a good part of his day meeting students standing by the vending machines in a corridor. Another has a mobile office parked in the basement garage but establishes a point of contact by selling coffee and doughnuts each morning. There is little resident life or sense of community on most campuses; students are generally part time and are involved in a limited way, "off and on." One campus minister compares his situation to being asked to provide a ministry at the local fast-food restaurant or filling station.

An exception may demonstrate the pattern. In one rural section of Iowa, local congregations built a traditional student center and campus ministry because the community college built a campus some distance from town with dormitories for students from widely scattered towns and farms in the district. For those students, the student center serves as a local church where no other is available. However, in most communities, the community college students who want to be church-related are already members of some local congregation. Congregational ministry with these students is that of the "home church."

Community colleges offer a particular challenge and opportunity to congregations. *First,* most congregations are located within the service district of some community college. (Note: In some states, branches of the state university or vocational-technical schools fulfill some of the functions of community colleges, and a separate community college system has not been developed.) *Second,* because few community colleges have campus ministers, it cannot be assumed that community college ministry is the responsibility of "the professionals." *Third,* the concerns of the congregation and the concerns of the community college are likely to overlap at many points as both are involved in service to the community. Both the community college and the congregation are institutions whose nature it is to give local, grass-roots expression to a larger ideal.

The Congregation Is Involved

Because the community college is a local institution, members of any congregation are likely to be involved with it. Church members may pay direct taxes or be asked to vote on bond issues for the college's support. They may serve on one of its many advisory committees or the board of trustees. They may be enrolled in a training program run by the community college or have attended a concert on campus. They may be attending classes in a degree program or have a member of the family enrolled. They may be working for the community college as an adjunct faculty member, a secretary, a maintenance person, or in some other role.

Members of the congregation may already be involved in community college ministry because of their ministry in the world as teachers, administrators, supporters of education, or students. Christian people minister as they do what they are called to do in the world. Many members of the congregation may also have what we might call a "pastoral" ministry with community college students as well. Community college students live in and are part of the community. They are ministered to by people on campus, in the congregation, in their homes, and in the community, perhaps more often by lay people than by the ordained leader of a congregation.

Student ministry with community college students is likely to be very different from images of traditional student ministry. Community college students tend to be "nontraditional" students. Many are part time and even the full-time students are likely to have other employment. Many students at the community college are the first in their families to attend college, and many are studying in technical rather than "academic" fields. Even those students who are taking a full load of classes are not apt to think of themselves as "college students."

The older community-college student's involvement with education may not seem to make much difference for pastoral ministry. But education changes people, and almost everyone who turns to the community college is in some process of transition. Transition points in life tend to be when people most need and are most open to ministry. The challenge for pastors, ordained and lay, is to be alert to where people are changing and growing, and to help individuals integrate new learnings and self-concepts into their understandings of themselves before God.

Opportunities for ministry are created by the function of the community college as a community service agency. The community college conceives of itself as having a "mission"; it serves the community, helping people learn and grow and making education democratically available. Congregations that understand a part of their own mission to include improving the quality of human life, aiding people to achieve equal opportunity, or promoting the growth of individuals and groups within their communities will often find the community college an ally. A small sampling of the programs that have been jointly developed by churches and community colleges include:

- workshops, classes, and seminars on aging, death and dying, being single, world hunger, family life, etc.;
- career counseling services and vocational testing for people at a community crisis center;
- placement of volunteers in human service agencies as part of a training program;
- creation of day care facilities and the accreditation of child care workers;
- community programs in the humanities; and
- training programs for church volunteers in
  —church music,
  —developmental needs of children,
  —management of volunteers.

In some cases the resources of the community college have been brought to the church. In other cases the churches have brought special resources to the community college. In many cases, both have worked to create a service for someone else. Such cooperation may be initiated by a single individual or committee within a congregation that has a special concern. In one case, a woman concerned about local resources for retarded children found that she could not get volunteers in her congregation for a project until she had enlisted the support of some people who were teaching human resources development at the college. Many times congregations that have become active in a community concern have discovered that the community college is already at work.

For congregations that are concerned about the entire community in which they are located, it is as natural to be involved with the governance of the community college as with the local hospital, school board, or referendum on public housing. As in other areas of public life, it *does* make a difference who serves on the local board of trustees or governors, and it cannot be assumed that they are all good-hearted, wise, and dedicated to the public good.

> In your community is there a local board? Who serves on it? Are members elected or appointed? Are there regular meetings open to the public? Who serves on the various advisory committees of the college?

Numerous decisions made at state and local levels determine the allocation of resources in the community college, who will be served, what will be taught, and what will be permitted. Because most community colleges are community institutions dependent in part on local support, they are generally very responsive to local pressure. At times this responsiveness to local pressure can be a liability that restricts academic freedom and an inclusive vision, and the community college may need in the religious community an ally that will speak on its behalf. As an example, in one community, church members became advocates against a policy that would have excluded international students, because they felt that personal contact with people from other countries was an important part of the kind of education that the church wanted to promote.

The community college may need the help of concerned citizens and church people to help the institution wrestle with some of the issues which it faces, such as:

- How can local control and responsiveness be retained when funding of the college comes from state-level increases?
- How can the college best respond to nontraditional learners so that the "open-door" admissions policy does not become a revolving door?
- How can community colleges resist the machinations of those who would make of the community college a "second-class system" into which minorities can be tracked?
- How can community colleges attract and retain faculty who understand the special role of the community college and who want to pursue the challenge of undergraduate teaching?

It has been said that in our society people turn to education when they want change and to the churches when they want stability. At their best, community colleges help people become more productive, more self-reliant, and more open to an enlarged vision of the world; at the same time, some people feel that the church has encouraged them to be dependent, passive, and limited in vision. The story may also be told in reverse. There are those who have looked to the community college with high hopes and have found it an impersonal and difficult institution that added to their sense of failure. Both the church and the community college are institutions that can fall short of their high goals and sense of mission. Both can benefit from the prophetic voice of reform and from those who point out the difference between the real and the ideal.

Developing Your Ministry

You can become acquainted with the community college in many ways. If you visit on campus, take a course, or sit in on a meeting of the trustees, you will see a *part* of the college. Remembering the story of the blind men and the elephant (how each man had a distorted impression of the animal as a whole because of his assumptions about the small part that he had experienced), don't assume that you understand the community college. It is a new kind of animal, diversified in its mission (which even its staff doesn't always understand), and its local manifestations are often very different from one another. Enrollments may be anywhere from two hundred to fifty thousand students. The community college may have no buildings of its own or be spread over several campuses. Faculty and administrators are apt to be unlike any academic types you have ever met: instructors from many different professions, second careerists formerly in the military or the ministry, Ph.D.s who came to the community college out of a commitment to undergraduate teaching, and professional administrators who may never have taught but speak a strange jargon of "FTEs" (Full-Time Equivalents) and "curriculum articulation."

If you are a pastor of a congregation, you may find that the community college is more accessible and provides more direct assistance than most institutions of higher education because of its orientation to the local community. If you want to see the president or ask to speak to the board of trustees, it will be assumed that as pastor of a congregation you have some important local constituency, so you are likely to be listened to. With a mandate to assist local groups, the director of community services will be willing to listen to you when you come to talk about a possible project. If you have laid the groundwork by getting to know people, the affirmative action officer in the personnel department will thank you when you refer potential job candidates. The admissions counselor will welcome the opportunity to speak to your high school group because local recruitment is part of the task.

The community college can be a resource for ministry with individuals. It can provide a testing ground for the younger student unsure about future plans, training for the individual needing to retool for mid-life employment, enrichment for the retired, and remedial education for the disadvantaged. Those who counsel and work with people in the congregation and the community need to be informed about what resources the community college has to offer and on whom to call in order to best help others use the available resources.

The development of relationships between college leadership and a team of leaders from the religious community has proved an effective way of meeting student needs and other concerns for ministry. The community college is part of, and must be sensitive to, a pluralistic culture, and most responsible personnel at community colleges prefer to deal with an ecumenical or interfaith group of religious leaders.

Cooperative, voluntary ministries seem to work best at smaller community colleges, in towns and rural areas where people naturally have some sense of shared community. Around large campuses in urban areas it is often more difficult for clergy and college personnel to know one another. In these areas, it has proved helpful to have a paid "campus ministry associate" serving part time who can become knowledgeable about the institution, facilitate the activities of local churches, and provide a point of contact for students. (This method has two potential dangers. *First,* congregations often feel that "it's all taken care of" when staff is hired and miss the larger benefits of relating to the community college. *Second,* there tend to be expectations that with staff present an "old-fashioned" campus ministry centered on a student group will emerge. These expectations are usually both frustrating and frustrated. They miss the point that the "communitycollege" is both a college and an agency.)

EXERCISE: Church and "Communitycollege"

The survey below was developed by the Reverend Mark Rutledge of Albuquerque, New Mexico. It is reprinted with his permission.

Local Church/Community College Survey

1. Has your congregation been involved in any kind of cooperative programs with the community college(s) in your district?

   _____yes _____no

2. If yes, please specify what.
3. Are you related to the college in any way, e.g., as part-time faculty, volunteer, student?

   _____yes _____no

4. If yes, please specify.
5. Are there members of your congregation who are on the faculty or staff of the community college?

   _____yes _____no _____don't know

6. If yes, have you talked or worked with them in developing programs or ministries with the college?

   _____yes _____no. If yes, please specify.

7. Are there members of your congregation who are students at the community college?

   _____yes _____no _____don't know

8. If yes, have you worked with them in any kind of way? Please specify.

9. Do you have any relationship with the college through its office of community services?

   _____yes _____no. If yes, please specify.

10. Do you have any contacts with the college through their office of student personnel services?

    _____yes _____no. If yes, please specify.

11. Is religion taught at the college, either in separate courses or as part of existing courses in humanities, philosophy, or another department?

    _____yes _____no _____don't know

12. If yes, are you involved in any way in teaching?

13. Are members of your church related to the college in any other way, e.g., as a member of an advisory committee or trustee?

    _____yes _____no _____don't know

14. Does the college provide resources to the churches in your area, e.g., workshops, adult education seminars, training for religious educators?

    _____yes _____no __________don't know. If yes, please specify.

15. Does the church provide resources to the college such as building space, volunteer time, or support in the community?

    _____yes _____no. If yes, please specify.

16. Do the church and the college work together to provide services to people in your community?

    _____yes   _____no. If yes, please specify.

17. Is there interaction between the college and other denominations or churches in your district, such as Roman Catholic, Lutheran?

    _____yes   _____no. Specify.

18. Are you interested in working or continuing to work in this area?

    _____yes   _____no

For Further Reading—Community College and Local Church

Gleazer, Edmund J., Jr., *The Community College: Values, Vision and Vitality*. Washington, D.C.: American Association of Community and Junior Colleges, 1980. $6.50. The above is a review of current and future directions for the community college from one of the experts in the field. Available from the National Center for Higher Education, American Association of Community and Junior Colleges, One Dupont Circle, N.W., Washington, DC 20036.

The following are available from the United Ministries in Education Communication Office, % Educational Ministries, American Baptist Churches, Valley Forge, PA 19481.

The Butterfly Connection: An Evaluative Report on Campus Ministry with Community Colleges in Southern California, 1967–79. $2.50. This report shares what was learned by a community college ministry project during its years of organizing and implementation of ministry.

Hallman, William E., ed., *The Challenge of the Community College to the Church*. 1980. $4 prepaid. Produced by the Community College Program of the United Ministries in Education.

____________________, *So There's a Community College in Your Town*. Rev. ed. 1978. $3 prepaid. Produced by the Community College Program of the United Ministries in Education.

Community College and Local Church

Live Wire is a guide for local committees working with community college ministry, geared to nonstaff situations.

"Perspectives on the Church and the Community College" are occasional papers published several times annually.

Additional materials are available from the United Ministries in Education Community College Program, 848 Pittock Block, 921 S.W. Washington Street, Portland, OR 97205.

Chapter 7

College and Congregation in Mission

The Dallas County Community College District is spread over seven campuses in the midst of an urban population of over a million people. Part-time campus ministers on five of the campuses provide a focal point for ministry and link local congregations with the colleges.

The campus ministry provides resources for the churches. On one campus, a Friday evening program for singles draws together people from area churches that each have a small number of young single people. No one church could do it alone, but through cooperation with campus ministry they can have a significant program. The campus ministry has helped the college produce a "Singles' Saturday" program, with a variety of workshops for single people, which 350 people attended. The campus ministry brought in a program on voluntary simplicity concerning "Alternative Celebrations," which was presented on several campuses and in local churches. The campus ministry also helps bring community college resources to the churches. With campus ministry help, the college created a course on "Coping with Aging" that was offered in several local churches.

Campus ministry brings the resources of the churches to the campus. In one instance, local congregations identified clergy and lay people with special areas of expertise who were willing to speak in appropriate classes. In another project, local clergy are being sought both to provide counseling services and to learn new skills at a proposed family services center on one campus. In yet another project, lay volunteers are being sought to provide hospitality for a short-term program of bringing exchange students from abroad.

The Dallas County Community College Ministry was begun with the support of the Dallas Council of Churches. It has the continued support of that agency and a number of regional church judicatories. Clusters of twenty to thirty congregations are linked to the campus closest to them through an advisory council, and individual churches are linked to the campus ministry directly. Each congregation is asked to enter into a covenant with the campus ministry, pledging to inform the campus ministry about their own events and the names of students, faculty, and staff from the congregation, as well as to give financial support to the ministry.

There is a high degree of partnership, mutual support, and cooperation between this campus ministry and the congregations in Dallas, Texas. If we can discover what works in the program in Dallas, we can learn from this in order to promote such partnerships in other places. What are the elements of cooperation? Some of the structural factors we can identify as follows:

1. **A Two-Way Street**—Congregations are not just the funders or providers of a ministry that is sent to the campus. The congregations help with the campus ministry and campus ministry staff help congregations with their programs. The colleges are also a part of this mutual ministry.

2. **Personal Involvement**—People from the participating congregations are directly involved in carrying out the ministry, both in their congregations and on campus. The campus ministry provides for them a way to be directly involved in short-term commitment or one-time programs where their particular gifts can be used. Campus ministers are involved in activities in the congregations, known to pastors, and invited to preach.

3. **Localism**—While the Dallas County Community College Ministry serves a very large area, congregations are involved in a committee and in activities that focus on the community college in their district.

4. **An Ecumenical Vehicle**—The campus ministry does not have to spend large amounts of energy encouraging interchurch cooperation, establishing credibility, or creating an ecumenical agency, because it has the continuing support of the already existing Council of Churches.

5. **Congregational Ownership**—Many congregations are associated with the campus ministry through their denominations, but they do not have to rely on this sometimes tenuous connection. The governing

board of each local congregation is asked to consider its relationship to the campus ministry through the covenanting process.

6. **Regional Staff—**The only full-time staff person for the Dallas County Community College Ministry is the Reverend Betsy Turecky. Her major job is facilitating the overall cooperation of church, college, and campus ministry. Her considerable energy, vision, and charisma play an important role in Dallas, a factor that cannot be reproduced in other places. What can be learned and applied other places is that she did not approach the churches as a campus minister trying to gain support for a program. She approached both church and college with a vision of mutual cooperation, seeking their involvement in bringing this about. Her skills are not those of a traditional campus minister, but those of an enabler.

Partnership with the College

The Dallas County Community College Ministry represents a partnership not only with local churches, but also with the community college. This partnership begins with some commonality of purpose. The Dallas County Community College District speaks of itself as being "in mission" to the community. The Community College Ministry sees itself as in mission *with* the community college and the churches, serving human needs in the community.

In Jacksonville, Florida, the churches and universities associated with the Jacksonville Campus Ministry have identified at least three important goals which they share in common. Both institutions are committed to the following goals:

1. To discover and make known truth;
2. To help persons develop their full potentiality as human beings;
3. To utilize their resources to improve the quality of life in their communities.

Recognition of common goals has led to a variety of cooperative program offerings including:

- a forum on southern Africa attended by persons from several local churches and led by three Jacksonville University faculty members;
- a four-session "Going to College Seminar" for local church senior highs and their parents resourced by university student personnel staff;

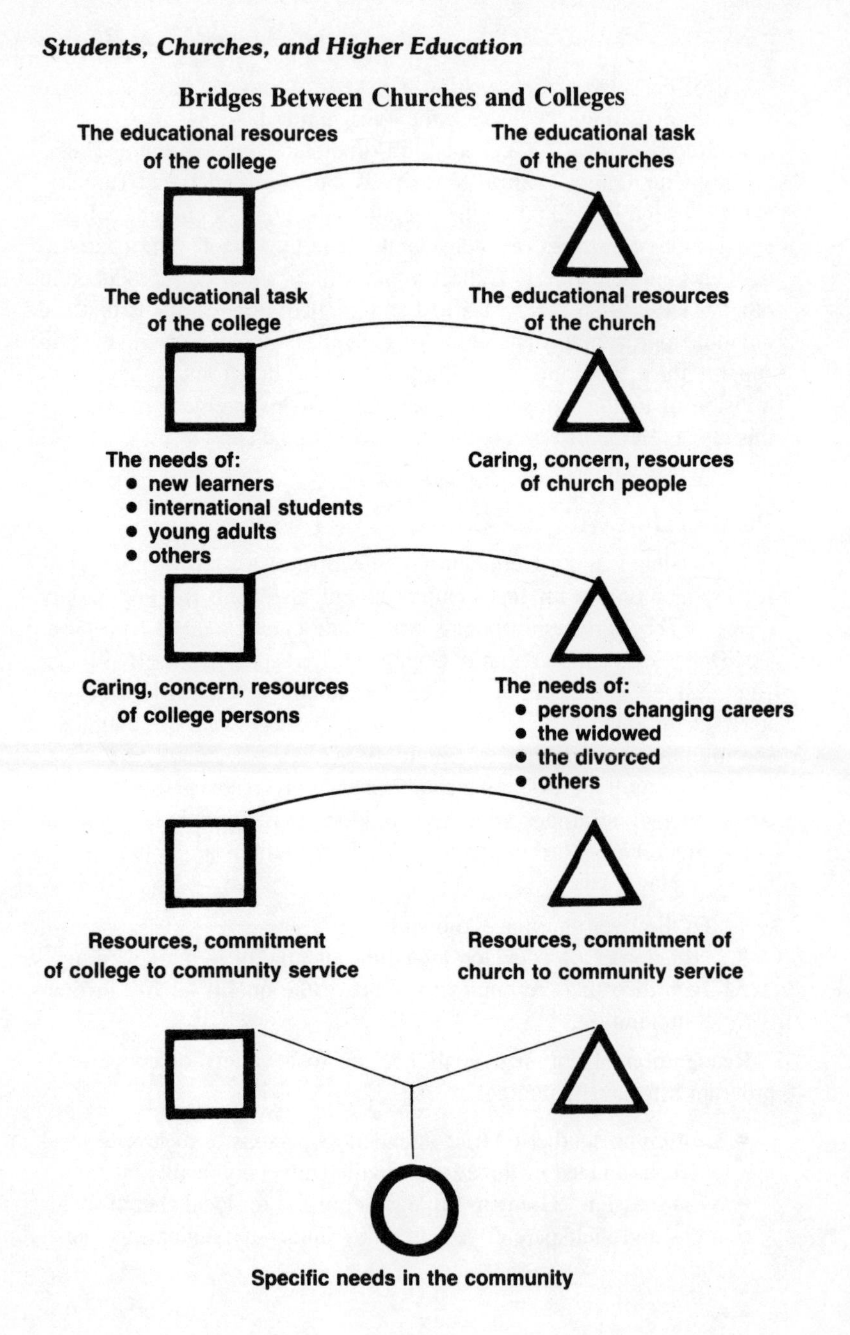
Bridges Between Churches and Colleges
The educational resources of the college
The educational task of the churches
The educational task of the college
The educational resources of the church
The needs of:
• new learners
• international students
• young adults
• others
Caring, concern, resources of church people
Caring, concern, resources of college persons
The needs of:
• persons changing careers
• the widowed
• the divorced
• others
Resources, commitment of college to community service
Resources, commitment of church to community service
Specific needs in the community

- a credit course at the University of North Florida on ''The Meaning of Death'' taught by a team composed of the campus minister and two other faculty members and utilizing local religious leadership;
- a noncredit course on ''Teaching Skills in Religious Education'' offered by university education faculty for church school teachers;
- an ''Evening of Exploration into Changing Roles for Women and Men'' and a workshop on ''Coping with Change in the Family'' for a suburban community, utilizing the combined resources of a local church and a university; and
- a noncredit course at Jacksonville University on ''Spiritual and Psychic Experience'' coordinated by the campus minister and utilizing local religious leadership.

In Jacksonville, the campus ministry is a linking agency, or bridge, to help bring together the needs and resources of colleges and congregations. Robert Thomason, the director of that ministry, provides a schematic drawing (shown on page 110) of bridges which can be built.

These bridges, or partnerships, between college and congregation can be built without a professional campus ministry. The Reverend J Springer has developed and extensively tested a process to initiate cooperation between the religious leadership in a community and local colleges. The goal of the process is to discover and establish a variety of mutually enriching relationships between religious congregations and nearby colleges.

The process can begin with one interested person on campus or in the community familiarizing himself or herself with the Tool Kit and Handbook Springer has prepared. Particularly important is ''Tool Kit #1'' (page 1 of the Tool Kit), reproduced with Springer's permission.

A COLLEGE AND THE RELIGIOUS COMMUNITY
THE PROMISE OF MUTUAL BENEFIT

COLLEGE ARENAS	SUGGESTED COLLABORATION OF RELIGIOUS AND COLLEGE LEADERS
Admissions	1. Initiating a minimum child play center so young mothers in the community might attend college. 2. Annual ''update'' on the college for the area clergy with particular focus on the programs of the college which ''minister'' to the edu-

cationally or economically disadvantaged.

Career Counseling	1. Use of career counselors in life planning and career choice in high school religious conferences-retreats. 2. Workshop for clergy to update them on tools and trends in career and life planning.
Counseling	Cataloguing those clergy skilled in counseling for referral purposes, and for occasional use as resource personnel for in-service training of both students and staff. A holistic approach to the student is therefore provided.
Student Activities	Provide opportunities whereby students can converse with religious leaders on current issues. These could be "piggyback" discussions following existing programs such as the film or theatre series. Or, they could be a special series on "How My Beliefs Have Changed" or "What Gives Me Hope for the Future" with cosponsorship coming from one of the departments of the college.
Credit Courses	Cataloguing the expertise/interests of religious leaders in a brochure to be shared with faculty so that the latter might occasionally involve them in the classroom as guest lecturers. Since religious issues/topics rise again and again throughout much of the curriculum, the use of religious leaders would not be an imposition upon the subject matter.
Continuing Education	1. Explore strategies which would enable local congregations to be more aware of the opportunities at the college for their personal self-renewal and growth. 2. Are there courses which religious leaders might offer, such as Death and Dying, Religious Themes in Cinema? 3. What courses might be offered *to* religious leaders for their professional and skill development? Workshops in Life Planning, Creative Problem Solving, Organizational Development might be of interest.
Community Services	Compile a list of pressing needs in the community or county, prioritize them, list the resources that are available or could be made available, and explore those which the college and the religious community might address together.

Governance — Enable religious leaders to understand how the college is governed and knowledgeable about the variety of forces both internal and external which impinge upon the college. For example, why are certain courses offered? Who decides the cost per course? Is there a quota operating in terms of admissions? What is the impact of the state?

THE VISION? — Colleges and Local Religious Communities can be institutions without Walls, having Open Doors to one another and to the community at large. Each can enrich and enable the other and the community.

NO WALLS:

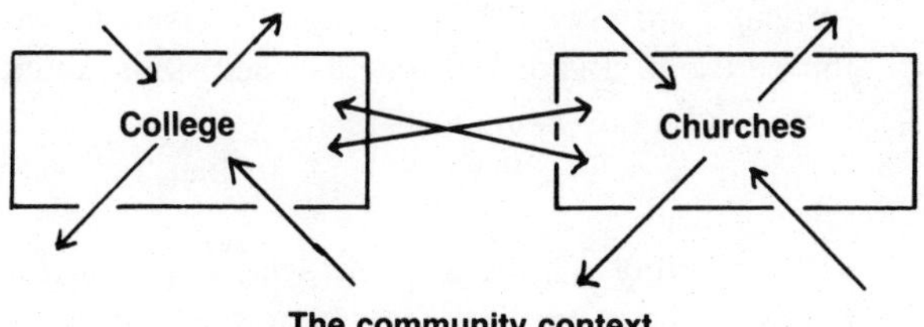

From one interested individual, the process proceeds to the local ministers' association or other ecumenical or interfaith body in the community. "Tool Kit #1" is used to raise consciousness about the kinds of relationships which are possible and which are occurring in other places. From the ecumenical or interfaith group, an Exploration Team of four to six persons is created to explore with the college ways in which the college and the religious community can enrich each other.

The third step in the Springer method is to interpret to the college the decision and intent of the interfaith group, again using "Tool Kit #1." The Exploration Team requests that a staff person from the college join them in designing a day of visitation on campus. This planning meeting is a fourth step. As a fifth step, the Exploration Team spends a structured day on campus to learn more about the college and to explore with college personnel the notion that the college community and the religious community can be mutually resourceful.

In most places where this method has been tried, the Exploration Team discovered some people on campus who were interested in the possibilities of cooperation in particular areas. Some of the interested people from the college, as well as some from the religious community, created an ongoing Ecumenical Higher Education Task Force. No program as such was created, but the task force provided a bridge by means of which there could be cooperation in those arenas where there was interest. It is not expected that the Springer method will result in cooperation in every arena. Cooperation requires interest on both sides of the bridge, and an exchange of resources as well.

This simple bridge-building method has several particular advantages which Springer points out:

- It allows volunteers with limited time and energy a way of focusing their energy in one or two areas. Volunteers can pursue those particular areas where they have interests or talents. Possibilities for the use of a variety of interests and skills are created (not just those relating to young students).
- The holistic nature of the Judeo-Christian tradition is affirmed by this approach.
- The possibility is created for two-way traffic, and it is recognized that the college can be a resource to the church.[1]

Some of the ways in which the college can be a resource to the church are suggested by a tool created by Robert Thomason of Jacksonville, mirroring Springer's "Tool Kit #1" (used with Thomason's permission):

ARENAS	SUGGESTED RESPONSES BY COLLEGES TO CHURCH NEEDS
Missions	1. Seminar on current mission theme—e.g., southern Africa, Caribbean. 2. Resource directory of persons from other countries.
Education	1. Course on "Teaching Skills in Religious Education." 2. Consultant services for planning curriculum, administering a comprehensive educational program, etc. 3. Bible courses.
Youth Ministry	"Going to College Seminar" for senior highs and their parents.

[1]J Lynn Springer, *Handbook,* p. 3. Consult "For Further Reading," chapter 5, for availability.

Children's Ministry	Consultant services and student intern placements for church kindergartens, day care centers.
Worship	1. Computers and consultant services for congregational worship survey. 2. "Religion and the Arts" series. 3. Performers for church music groups.
Counseling	1. Mid-life career change counseling for church persons. 2. Counseling skills training for clergy.
Social Concerns	Seminars on contemporary social issues—e.g., "Changing Roles for Women and Men" and "Crisis in the Family."
Stewardship	Consultant services re: budget planning, fund raising, etc.
Administration	Consultant services re: organizational development, program planning, etc.
Evangelism	Computer and consultant services for surveying the community.

Both Thomason and Springer agree that the success of mutual ministry lies in discovering how church and college can assist each other in their ongoing tasks. Springer speaks of a strategy of "seasoning the center," using volunteers in activities in which the church or college already has a stake. This is much easier, he says, then trying to create new cocurricular programs, an approach he refers to as "hustling on the sidelines." In order to keep focused on the center, and to have a volunteer partnership succeed, he says it is essential to ask and reask the right questions. (See the following exercise.)

EXERCISE: College and Congregation in Mission

Consider the following questions. (It is J Springer's insight that we must keep asking the "big question." This particular formulation of that question as a threefold question, including a mutual concern for the community, derives from Robert Thomason.)

1. What are the ways in which the college can be resourceful and enriching to the people and institutions of the religious community?

2. What are the ways in which the religious community can be resourceful and enriching to the people and structures of the college?

3. How can the colleges and churches, working together, be resourceful and enriching to the persons and structures of the community?

For Further Reading—College and Congregation in Mission

The Church and the Community College in Mission. Available for rental from the United Ministries in Education Communication Office, % Educational Ministries, American Baptist Churches, Valley Forge, PA 19481. $10 plus postage. A slide and cassette program about the Dallas County Community College Ministry.

Hallman, W. E., ed., *The Challenge of the Community College to the Church.* Valley Forge: United Ministries in Education, 1980. $4. See especially chapter 7, "A Plan for Mission: A Description of the Jacksonville Campus Ministry."

McGown, David J., and Creel, Marilyn K., *The Workbook: Local Community Parish and Local Community College Interaction.* Available from Community College Project, Agape House, 1064 West Polk Street, Chicago, IL 60607. $3.

Springer, J, *Handbook/Tool Kit.* See "For Further Reading" in chapter 5 for availability.

Chapter 8

Partnerships with Campus Ministry

In many places, the church has provided specialized and professional ministers on campus as a way of carrying out ministry with higher education. These campus ministers can be a resource for the congregation's ministry, and the support can be mutual. For this mutual support to occur, bridges need to be built. While campus and congregational ministries are both engaged in the mission of the church, their settings for ministry differ. Understanding these differences is a first step in bridge building. Understanding the different forms of ministry is also essential for the congregation or the pastor considering ministry on the campus.

> "The parish on the whole deals with persons in their personal and family relations. When I was a college chaplain, while I was dealing with my share of those personal and family issues, the context was entirely different—not the home, but the work place—for students, and even more so for faculty.
>
> "My pastoral ministry was with professional men and women as related to their functions in institutions, and dealt, therefore, continually with institutional issues. This meant getting into social ethics: questions of power, of economics, and of politics. . . ."[1]

The reflections above were written by John Crocker on the occasion of his move from being a campus minister to being the pastor of a congregation in a university town.

In general, we can characterize some important differences between congregational and campus ministry thus:

[1]John Crocker, Jr., "Switching Mentalities: From Campus to Parish," *The Witness*, vol. 61, no. 11, p. 16.

Congregational ministry tends:	Campus ministry tends:
• to deal with people where they reside, in terms of their personal and family life.	• to deal with people at their place of work and study.
• to deal with those who congregate, who seek affiliation with the church.	• to deal with many people not actively affiliated with the church.
In the congregation, especially in worship:	**On the campus:**
• members are lay people (or the laity).	• clergy are generally lay people dealing with professionals in many fields.
• people assume an attitude of dependence on another (directed towards God, but often manifested towards other people).	• people operate out of their own sense of competence (intra-dependence).
• people engage in symbolic activity (related to basic assumptions, global images, primary process thinking).	• people engage in work activity (related to goals, rationality, secondary process thinking).
The pastor of a congregation:	**The campus minister:**
• spends a major amount of time with people who share similar beliefs.	• works in a pluralistic setting with many who don't share his or her basic assumptions.
• has a leadership role among the people with whom he or she works.	• is marginal, without a central or clearly defined role in the institution.
• has a responsibility for the maintenance of the institution.	• is in some ways a free agent, a missionary.

These differences and others can sometimes get in the way of easy partnership between congregations and campus ministers. People who stay in campus ministry tend to be those who like the academic setting. They may be more at home with college professors than with the mix of people in congregations. They may seem more oriented to issues than to people. They may be more concerned with the theoretical than the practical. Because of the context of their work they are likely to be more attuned to the needs of the world than to issues within the church and alert to some needs and issues talked about in the academy which have not yet gained widespread popular awareness. All of these factors may also be part of the gift which campus ministry can bring to enrich the life of the congregation. In turn, campus ministry needs to hear the concerns that ordinary practical people from many walks of life have within and for the life of the church.

Sometimes structural factors separate campus and congregational ministries. Many campus ministries are ecumenical, related to several denominations, while the congregation has most of its contacts within one denominational structure. Campus ministers are seldom directly accountable to one congregation but report to an ecumenical agency or to a committee within the denominational structure. Yet many campus ministers want to be accountable and of service to congregations and say, "I see myself as an assistant on the staff of every congregation in the region, ministering on their behalf."

All too frequently, congregations and campus ministries have been alienated. Both have felt misunderstood and unsupported by the other. The factors that created this situation are largely rooted in the past, in the separation of residential colleges from the mainstream of society and in the antagonism between campuses and large segments of American society in the 1960s. The world of higher education is now less separated from the community it serves, and congregations are increasingly involved with people engaged in higher education. The time is ripe for new partnerships between congregation and campus in ministry.

Church-Linked Campus Ministry

The Wesley Foundation and Wesley United Methodist Church in Charlottesville are linked by a short gravel path connecting their back doors. They say that it is a symbol of their relationship, united in sometimes rocky and tenuous ways. The director of the Wesley Foundation frequently leads Sunday worship at the church where most of the congregation is university related. Students make up a large part of the worshiping congregation, and university resource people are sometimes used in adult forums. But the church and the foundation are separate entities, with separate governing boards and different ministries.

The campus minister and the pastor admit that they deal with many of the same people, but in different ways. The pastor says, "I do see the faculty and staff, but I usually see them in the context of family, and not necessarily as faculty and staff. My relationship to them tends to be as a pastor to a family." In contrast, there is a faculty breakfast at the foundation which deals with university concerns, and the campus minister works with many faculty on campus in the context of their jobs.

Students are integrated into the program of Wesley United Methodist Church, but the foundation has been more successful in creating a student fellowship and mutual support group. The pastor visits some students on campus, generally out of some contact which has occurred Sunday morning, while the campus minister says, "The people to whom I relate include a lot of folks who have, at this period in their lives, decided not to be so very active in a congregation, and we don't see them on Sunday morning. Few people ever come here asking for the United Methodist campus minister. They always come because someone else referred them or some contact, very tentative contact, has been established outside of the office."

The congregation's program includes what the pastor calls such "churchy, middle-class, American things" as a big picnic and reception for students in September. The foundation, in contrast, has a diverse ministry. Approximately ninety different university, community, and church groups use its facilities. The campus minister comments, "It would take a very open congregation to host the variety of groups which use these facilities."

The connection with the campus ministry is sometimes difficult. Church members have left the congregation because of things in which the Wesley Foundation was involved. The pastor and the campus minister are accountable to different agencies, and so their cooperation with each other is voluntary. Sometimes relationships become strained, and there were times in the past, with different personnel, when there was no cooperation. What makes the situation work now is both the commitment both parties have to working together and the commitment of both the congregation and the campus ministry to the university as a major arena for ministry.

Yoked Ministries

A man or woman called to be both pastor of a congregation and a campus minister is being called to two different tasks. Time spent on campus with the unchurched doing unchurchy things will need interpretation to the congregation. A pastor or associate given the task of campus ministry is also likely to experience a tension between work on campus and work with the congregation. A particularly difficult situation may be created when a regional church judicatory has funds for a part-time campus ministry and creates a position linked part time to a local congregation. If the congregation is small and has only one paid staff person, there is frequently resentment about not having the services of a minister full time. In a multiple staff congregation, the campus ministry task is often assigned to a young associate with no experience in campus ministry who does not stay long enough to develop credibility. In either case, when the job is designed as a "fifty-fifty" split with one accountability to the congregation and one to an outside agency, schizophrenia and resentments are built in.

A yoked ministry *does* work where the congregation sees the university as its ministry, and the senior minister has the responsibility to be both pastor and campus minister. That can form a coherent whole, and the congregation and pastor together are accountable to the judicatory where that is necessary. Another arrangement that works, though less well, is to develop one responsibility, such as the pastorate, as primary, with a contract written for a specific number of hours to be spent in campus ministry.

The unity of congregational and campus ministry is workable whenever the mission is understood to be a whole. The First Baptist Church in North Brentwood, Maryland, is seven miles from the University of Maryland in College Park. The area is heavily populated, and the First Baptist Church is a large congregation with only a few members connected with the university. However, the congregation is happy to have their pastor serve as the campus minister for the Black Ministries Program at the university, because they have always understood their pastor to be a minister for the whole black community. Congregational members help provide transportation for those students who want to worship with them at the church (many do, and many do not). As a campus minister, the pastor draws together people on the campus for worship in the black tradition several times a year, as well as assisting with cultural festivals and a gospel choir. He serves as an advocate and counselor for black students on a campus which is predominantly white, and the congregation strongly supports him spending time with that. Because he is deeply involved in the community as well, and respected by the leaders of other congregations, he was able to bring congregations in the community together for an Easter sunrise service at the university chapel, another sign of the possible unity of ministry between the campus and the community.

In some places, congregations have responded to on-campus need by creating an agency for ministry on campus separate from the congregation. In Canton, Ohio, fifty-five local congregations created Interfaith Campus Ministry, Inc., to provide a campus ministry at the combined campuses of Stark Technical College and Kent State University (Stark Campus). The congregations provide money and representation on the corporation board to support an active ministry staff located on campus. The difficulty in this, and many similar situations, is that the campus ministry becomes unrelated to the local churches. Congregations, assuming that they have provided for campus ministry, fail to put effort into providing that kind of congregational ministry to students that only they can undertake. The ministry created by nine local churches (and two colleges) in Jacksonville, Florida, attempts to overcome some of these problems by having a central committee made up of lay people from the congregations and colleges, with a campus ministry enabler. Members of the central committee plan and carry out the ministry through task forces. Programs occur both on the campuses and in the congregations, with the campus ministry enabler being present on the campuses during the week and in one of the congregations on Sunday.

Regional Resources

Congregations can make use of the resource of campus ministry, even if they are geographically remote from a campus. Within every state and denomination there are campus ministers who can be reached by telephone. (See directory listed at end of chapter.) Some of the things which a congregation can do to use the resources of a campus minister are:

1. **Call the Campus Minister**—Get to know him or her personally as a way of building a bridge for future help. If one contact doesn't seem too helpful, ask if other campus ministers in the area or regional staff have a particular interest in providing resources to congregations.

2. **Ask for Program Resources**—Share with the campus minister your current concerns and program needs; often he or she will know someone on campus who may be able to speak to a group or provide other resources. Invite the campus minister to speak or preach in your congregation. Find out if the campus minister has areas of special skill or interest, and make a note for future reference.

3. **Swap Newsletters**—Put the campus minister on your congregation's mailing list to keep him or her in touch with what you are doing. Ask for brochures about the campus ministry and ask to be put on the mailing list for any newsletter which the campus minister may send out.

4. **Ask for Help in Your Ministry**—Ask if there are any resources in your area to help congregations which are involved in student or higher education ministries. Invite the campus minister to meet with you or a congregational committee to talk together about your congregation's ministry.

5. **Arrange a Visit to Campus**—If possible, plan to visit the campus minister on campus. If you have students on that campus, perhaps the campus minister can help you plan to visit them. If you are near the campus, ask if the campus minister could arrange a day for clergy or lay people to visit the campus and meet with key administrators or have a program about contemporary student concerns.

Your phone call to the campus minister is also a support of his or her ministry. It lets the campus minister know that someone "out there" cares, and gives the campus minister an opportunity to tell you something about the work on campus. Campus ministers need the support of congregations, and most welcome any opportunity to talk about and interpret their work.

Many of the objectives above could be accomplished with no more than a twenty-minute phone call. Out of such a contact, many more forms of cooperation might develop. In Blacksburg, Virginia, a traditional campus ministry at a residential college now hosts an annual conference to help promote mutual cooperation between churches and community colleges in the area and an orientation-to-college weekend for high school seniors. Other campus ministries have programs for parents, forums for high school students, drama groups, and choir programs which they take to congregations in their area.

Wherever you are and whatever form your ministry in higher education takes, there are probably individuals and networks of people available to help you. In many parts of the country specialists have the job of helping congregations develop their own ministry in and with higher education. Regional training events and consultations are held where pastors and lay people from local congregations can come together and find others who share common problems but bring different perspectives to enrich one another. Gatherings of campus ministers increasingly include part-time ministers and clergy from congregations in college towns. In some places ecumenical task forces can provide help with specific concerns such as community college ministry or ministry with minority groups in higher education. In addition, those in denominational offices who carry a portfolio for campus and higher education ministries have resources to support the ministry of congregations.

EXERCISE: A Variety of Ministries

What is the role of the local church in higher education ministry? We asked that question at a conference and got the following list of answers:

- worship, nurture, fellowship
- inclusion of students and faculty in church community
- to carry on theological education
- to raise ethical questions
- support of on-campus ministry
- to provide facilities for college activities
- welcoming international students in community
- allowing faculty to minister with their expertise in the local church setting.
- the congregation is a recipient of the educational process
- congregation provides matrix for education and growth
- fellowship for students
- to create dialogue groups around what is happening in the academic world
- to provide day care facilities
- theological and Bible study to equip students and faculty to minister
- to affirm expanding horizons of students away at college

What is the role of your congregation in higher education ministry? What might you add to the list above? What items already there could you check off as true in your congregation?

EXERCISE: Campus and Congregation

1. If you are in a college community, how do you think that your congregation is perceived by people on campus; what is the "word of mouth"?
2. Are there any people in your congregation who teach or work at a college? What are their names?
3. Is there a campus minister nearby? What other campus ministers do you know? How might you be mutually helpful to one another?

For Further Reading—Partnerships with Campus Ministry

Periodicals

Campus ministry is responsive to changes within higher education. One way to keep up with the changes on campus and in campus ministry is through newsletters and periodicals in the field, some of which are listed below.

The Circle is a packet of materials available through subscription from the Division of Campus Ministry and Educational Services, Lutheran Student Movement in the USA, Suite 1847, 35 East Wacker Drive, Chicago, IL 60601. Materials useful for the contact pastor in a college community are often included.

CSCM Yearbook is published by the Center for the Study of Campus Ministry, Valparaiso University, Valparaiso, IN 46383. A library of campus ministry materials is maintained at this center.

Higher Education News Notes is a quarterly newsletter available from the National Council of Churches, 475 Riverside Drive, New York, NY 10115. Contribution of $3 per year.

The NICM Journal for Jews and Christians is available quarterly to associates of the National Institute for Campus Ministries, 885 Centre Street, Newton Centre, MA 02159.

Students, Churches, and Higher Education

Toward Wholeness, the journal of Ministries to Blacks in Higher Education, is available through subscription from MBHE, % Elwyn D. Rawlings, Howard University, Box 822, Washington, DC 20059.

UME Connexion, the newspaper of the United Ministries in Education, is available from the United Ministries in Education Communication Office, % Educational Ministries, American Baptist Churches, Valley Forge, PA 19481. Subscription is $3 per year and includes four issues of *The UME Letter*.

Other Resources

Global Justice Resourcing Packet for Campus and Young Adult Ministries. Available from Global Justice Resourcing, National Division of the United Methodist Church, Room 320, 475 Riverside Drive, New York, NY 10015.

The following resources are available from the United Ministries in Education Communication Office, % Educational Ministries, American Baptist Churches, Valley Forge, PA 19481.

Directory of Ministers in Higher Education. $2. A list of all the campus ministers in eight participating denominations.

The United Ministries in Education *Resource Listing* is available free.

Other specialized organizations, newsletters, and resource listings in campus ministry do exist. Contact your nearest campus ministry or a denominational office for more information regarding your special interests.